The heart of
business success

How to overcome the Catch-22s of growing your business

Robert Copping

The heart of business success

First published in 2009 by;

Ecademy Press

6, Woodland Rise, Penryn, Cornwall, UK. TR10 8QD

info@ecademy-press.com

www.ecademy-press.com

Printed and Bound by; Lightning Source in the UK and USA

Set in Minion and Myriad Pro by Charlotte Mouncey

Graphics by Amanda Rymel of Viva Design and Marketing Ltd.

Printed on acid-free paper from managed forests. This book
is printed on demand, so no copies will be remaindered or
pulped.

ISBN 978-1-905823-52-9

Acknowledgements

To my wife Julia, whose continued support has been essential to the completion of this book and to my two daughters Eleanor Rose and Eva Grace who help me keep everything in perspective.

I would like to thank all the Sightpath Catalysts for their professional dedication and invaluable contributions to this project.

I would also like to acknowledge the many clients who have enabled me to develop the ideas presented in this book. Their entrepreneurial enthusiasm never ceases to inspire.

CONTENTS

Foreword by Vijay Patel

When I was 22 I had a shiny new degree in pharmacy, a burning ambition to start and build my own business and a need to borrow £6,000 to get me started! A succession of bank managers listened sympathetically to my enthusiastic plans, but the response was always the same: "No track record – No loan". But without the loan how could I get a track record? A classic Catch-22 position and the basis for Robert Copping's engaging new book.

Like many entrepreneurs I have never been a great enthusiast of academic theories, and Robert does not beat the reader down with a succession of business models, but gives solid practical advice based on real life examples. In reading this engaging volume I was reminded over and over again of the number of obstacles which have presented themselves to me in my career.

Over the last 35 years I have built several businesses, successfully and not so successfully, and if I had read a book like "The Heart of Business Success" I am confident that the outcome of my less successful ventures would have been different. The thought processes and steps which a business person has to take for a successful outcome are clearly detailed in this compelling and easy to read book.

No business is an island and Robert carefully maps out the many stakeholders that need careful and appropriate handling if they are not to inhibit the establishment and growth of a new business.

Each aspect of the business cycle is covered, from planning and entry through to growth and ultimately exit.

Successful entrepreneurial companies are the lifeblood of the world economy and Robert Copping's no nonsense advice makes this a compulsory read for entrepreneurs, aspiring entrepreneurs and successful business people at all stages of their careers.

Introduction

People who set up their own business are usually talented and motivated – so why do most fail to achieve any notable level of success?

Published statistics tell us that the odds of a new business succeeding are shocking. The best statistics that I've seen puts the chance of success at one in six for the UK and less than one in twenty for the United States. Both studies were conducted before the credit crunch of 2008, so future assessments are likely to be even worse.

This represents a terrible waste of time, money and talent; not only for the people involved but for the economy as a whole.

There's no shortage of books, advice and support for starting and running a business – but they don't tell you about the main dilemmas and Catch-22s you'll encounter and they certainly don't tell you how to overcome them.

In this context, a dilemma is a situation where you have a choice, but making the right choice at the right time can put you in a quandary.

For those who haven't read Joseph Heller's book, Catch-22, or seen Mike Nichols' film of the same name, the 'catch' refers to the conditions needing to be met by pilots before they could be excused flying combat missions over Italy during world war ll.

Catch-22 refers to a regulation that is essentially a circular argument. You could only be exempted from combat missions if you were insane <u>and</u> you requested it, yet if you requested it, you could not be insane – because you have to be sane to recognise your own insanity.

The term Catch-22 is now widely used to describe any situation where two actions are mutually dependent on the other action being completed first.

A familiar example occurs in the context of job searching – to apply for a job you require relevant work experience, yet to obtain the necessary work experience you need a relevant job.

The job searching example conveys the frustration of a Catch-22 and in order to overcome it you have to somehow break into its circularity – and that's not easy.

My work involves modelling businesses to help them plan for growth and in the course of this I'm continually aware of how almost everything in business seems to have some dependence on everything else.

So, it shouldn't surprise us to find the epitome of the circular argument, Joseph Heller's Catch-22, occurs several times when you try to grow a business.

But, just like everything else in business, these Catch-22s don't operate in isolation – they are also connected with each other. And this inter-dependence makes it even more difficult to break into them and overcome them.

I believe the dilemmas and Catch-22s described in this book contribute significantly to the high failure rates reported for businesses. I also believe that understanding them and planning how to overcome them is essential for your success.

If you're thinking of starting your own business or you've recently set up in business or you're about to embark on a growth phase – this book will help you succeed.

Given the figures, wouldn't you have to be crazy to set up your own business? Well, the fact that you're reading this book means that you recognise how difficult it is to succeed in business and therefore, you're probably not crazy.

When I first began modelling small businesses to help them plan how to succeed I experimented with various frameworks. It took many years of honing the design of the model before it finally emerged as the 'heart of business success.'

Since then the 'heart' model has been used to help many small businesses to quickly see the way ahead and plan how to get there.

The company I founded back in 2006, Sightpath Limited now has many Business Catalysts applying this process and enjoying the thrill of helping small businesses to become successful.

It doesn't matter what type of business you're in, understanding the dilemmas and Catch-22s of growing a business and how the heart model can be applied to help you overcome them will increase your chances of success.

Part 1 of this book introduces the various dilemmas and Catch-22s so that you quickly get to understand them and how they impact each other.

Part 2 introduces the 'heart of business success' and explains how you can apply it to make your dilemma decisions and break into the circularity of each Catch-22 to overcome them and increase your likelihood of success.

Part 3 develops the process to help you create your plan for success.

I've also included regular summaries to enable you to quickly revise the key points covered in each major section.

It only remains for me to wish you every success in your current venture and beyond.

If you would like further information about the subject of this book, please visit the web site:

www.theheartofbusinesssuccess.com

Part One

The Catch-22s of growing a business

What is success?

If your aim is to be successful and the aim of this book is to help you towards that success, we should begin by clarifying what success might mean; and in particular what success might mean for you.

We strive for success, but when we achieve it, we often need something more.

Success without some kind of significance tends to leave a void.

People who've been very successful usually crave significance. It adds purpose to their success.

Many people would like to make a difference in the world, although relatively few manage it.

This is because to be effective at making a difference you need to have reached a position of influence and that often comes as a result of success in your chosen field.

Some people manage to achieve success and significance within their chosen field, such as a scientist, a politician, a writer or even a journalist.

Others have to use the influence their success brings to make a difference in another way, for example:

- The film star who campaigns for freedom in a repressed country

- The sports person who gives up time to coach children in deprived areas

- The celebrity chef who campaigns to improve the diet of school children

- The business person who aims to cure disease in Africa.

You only have a certain amount of time to apply yourself and once you've chosen to direct your efforts towards a particular route, you may have to exclude the alternatives.

If you try to do too much, you are less likely to achieve success at any of them. You have to specialise. For example, you could be good at several sports, but to be great you have to focus on just one.

Everyone has a limited amount of attention because there are only twenty four hours in every day. Your attention has to be balanced across all the elements of your life that are important to you.

Usually this will be: family, fun and fitness coupled with success and significance.

Whilst none of these should be neglected at any point in your life, the proportion of your attention that each is given tends to change through your life.

A young family may take a very large slice of your attention at the expense of fitness and any significance beyond raising a family, whereas later in life when the immediate family has flown the nest, you often find that significance gets a larger slice of attention.

Try to imagine what you would love to do in terms of significance. Think of something that would continue to excite you rather than become routine.

It will give purpose to your expedition for success and help you feel good about striving for success because it will feel less like mere craving for personal greed.

Those that survive a disaster, such as a plane crash sometimes feel guilty that they managed to survive when many others perished. Especially, if they believe that others missed out because of their own tenacity to survive.

Similar subconscious feelings can exist when striving for success in your chosen field. These feelings can hold you back and reduce your chances of success.

If you have considered how your success is necessary in order for you to achieve significance, it will help to overcome any negative connotation.

Once you've identified your chosen field of significance, it may help you decide what additional expertise you might require. This is in addition to giving your time and money.

If you can recognise an area of expertise it will help you identify whether there is an alternative route to success that will give you a head start to your chosen field of significance.

For most of us, significance is not something we can indulge our imagination with until after we've achieved success. So, don't worry if you have no specific area of significance that you can identify now.

Just keep in your mind that you expect to do something with your success that will add purpose and provide significance.

This book is about success in business and that's what we'll explore now - what you do with that success is for another time.

What is success in business?

There is no right answer to defining success in business; it's what's right for you and your circumstances. It depends on your ultimate purpose, your attitude to risk and your level of ambition.

For the purposes of this book we will only consider business success that we can easily measure progress against.

I would like to propose that there are two universal measures of success in business that everyone can measure and compare:

1. Is your business providing you with an income greater than you could command working for another company?

2. What would someone else pay to buy your business?

The first measure of success can be an early target and a clear measure of your initial success.

The second measure is more of a ladder of success and can be measured at any rung. Ideally, the longer you've been running your business, the higher up the ladder you've climbed and the more your business is worth.

I believe that you are more likely to be successful if you focus on business valuation as the ultimate measure of business success.

Unfortunately, I see many business owners who have the desire to achieve great success in business, but don't even get close to our first measure never mind progressing along our second measure. They have all the stress and responsibility of employing and feeding others with work, but are never properly compensated for their efforts.

They might argue that it's worth it because they don't like working for anyone else, but that shouldn't mean they have to forego due reward for their efforts and get precious little quality time to devote to their own lives and families.

Generally, owners of small businesses have no real idea of what their business is likely to be worth and if they do venture a value they tend to over-estimate.

Let's compare your business to your home for a moment. I expect that you always keep an eye on the local market and have a reasonable idea of how much your house is worth. You wouldn't undertake any construction work on your house without understanding how it might affect its value. So why don't most owners of small businesses apply the same to their business? After all, it's potentially worth a lot more than your home and could secure a comfortable life in retirement without having to downsize your house.

Furthermore, Chief Executives of listed companies are judged against the company's share price and hence the business valuation, shouldn't your success also be judged by the value of your business?

If business value is the primary measure of success – that should be the focus of your decisions. Before making any major business decision, you should consider the likely impact on the value of your business.

As you read this book you may be quite surprised by the impact some decisions can have on the value of your business.

I believe that if you focus on business value from the outset, you're more likely to be one of the elite few to succeed.

The second measure of success can only be achieved if you create a business that someone is prepared to buy. This will usually, but not necessarily coincide with your exit from the business.

I think it's a good idea to consider your possible exit routes from the business right from the start because it can inform how you measure success and how you strive to achieve it.

It is also one of the most important questions asked by a potential investor: How and when do you plan to exit?

There are six common exit routes aside from the most likely exit, which is liquidation.

The term Liquidation doesn't necessarily mean that you've run into trouble and are forced to cease trading; it may be that you no longer want the company.

For example, you may have created a company as a vehicle for trading your own service and perhaps you want to retire and no longer require the business.

Alternatively, you may have been unsuccessful in your search for a buyer, so you decide to sell the assets, stop trading and choose to liquidate.

The purpose of this book is to help you to be successful in building your business to the point where it will be attractive as a purchase, so let's consider the other common exit routes:

1. Family inheritance

2. Management buy-out

3. Management buy-in

4. Merger

5. Trade Sale

6. Flotation.

Let's take a moment to review each of these in turn.

1. Family Inheritance

The precise valuation of the business is likely to be less important than what you've achieved during your tenure of the business. Your aim will also be to pass on the business in good health.

In the case of Family Inheritance a primary consideration is likely to be to minimise the payment of tax on the transfer of ownership. You may be able to wrap some of your shares in a trust fund if your children are inclined towards the business.

Whether you want family members to take active positions in the company or not, you will need to groom your successor. If there is more than one contender you will need time to explore which is the best option, so you will need to plan ahead for your exit.

2. Management buy-out

Where the business is offered for sale to another director or the existing management team you will probably want to get an independent valuation. You will also need to give them time to raise the finance so again you will need to plan ahead.

They might struggle to raise the finance and you may have to allow them to purchase the business in stages. In this case you will need to decide at what point you will exit. In the first year of transition you might feel that you wish to remain in control as the majority of your worth may still be tied up in the business.

3. Management buy-in

A management buy-in is when an external management team buys the business. Senior members of the team are likely to be taking a personal stake in the business, but they are usually backed by a venture capital company.

They may request that you remain with the business in a consultancy capacity for a short period to ensure a smooth hand-over. In this case, they are likely to defer payment for some of the shares.

You may also be required to sign a no-competition clause for several years to prevent you starting a similar business and poaching customers and employees.

4. Merger

Mergers are common with service-based business such as accountancy or law firms, especially if they complement each other in terms of services or geography.

A merger is likely to require your involvement to continue for a while and hence, it will not necessarily provide an immediate exit.

5. Trade Sale

The most likely purchaser of a small business is a competitor or someone wanting to get into your market. This is normally referred to as a trade sale.

A trade buyer's motivation for purchasing a business is probably one of the following:

1. To gain your market share and benefit from improved efficiency and profitability.

2. To obtain the expertise you have built up within your business.

3. To benefit from a product or service that you already have and your business is known for providing. This may refer to a patent or to distribution rights for somebody else's product or brand. It may also refer to a signed contract, particularly if the other party is the Government, a local authority, or a large corporation.

4. To cross-sell their range of products or services to your customer base.

To be a target for purchase, your business has to achieve a reasonable level of satisfaction for at least one of the buyer motivations listed above.

These buyer motivations help to understand why a business is initially worth very little. Until the effort of purchasing a business is outweighed by the benefit of that acquisition, a business can never achieve success against our second measure. It certainly won't be worth sufficient for the current owner to feel compensated for the time and money already invested.

Of course, just because someone would like to buy your business doesn't mean that you have to sell it. But wouldn't it be great to know that you have reached a level of success that can be recognised by your business peers?

6. Flotation

If you grow to a reasonable size, other options become possible such as floating the business on one of the smaller exchanges. Effectively, you're required to attract multiple buyers at the same time. You may have the option to remain with the company after flotation or you may decide this is the right time to exit.

Flotation is an exit strategy achieved by very few businesses because it usually means the business has strong earnings and significant growth prospects or scalability – this is covered in more detail later.

Speed of success

A refinement to the second measure of success is to include how quickly a particular business valuation was achieved. The faster you achieve your desired success the more time you'll have available to apply your resources to a new venture and achieve even greater success.

Most business owners have at least one other idea knocking around in their head, but their commitment to the present business means they usually don't have the time to progress it.

Only when you've actually sold a business will you have a true measure of the value of it, but then you have no further opportunity to grow it.

So, the clearest measure of success that can be universally compared before you've actually sold your business is an estimate of what your business is currently worth.

That's why I recommend you work out a means to monitor the valuation of your business and be able to check how a business decision might affect the valuation before you commit to it. Various methods of business valuation are discussed in Part 2.

As we continue we'll explore some of the difficulties of starting and growing a business and how to use the heart model to overcome them to achieve greater business success more quickly.

Now we know what we mean by success, let's take a moment to reflect on the way a business tends to grow and the importance of cash in achieving growth.

Business Phases

Most businesses that survive the perilous start-up phase will eventually run into some kind of limitation. This may be self-imposed in that you don't want to grow beyond a certain size. Or it may be that the market and the competition within that market means that it isn't commercially viable to grow beyond a certain share of that market. And the relevant market might be local, national or even global.

This means that a simplistic representation of the way a business develops is the 'S' curve showing three phases: start-up, growth and maturity.

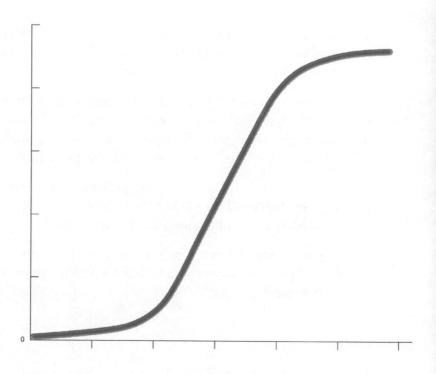

Business growth curve

Start-ups grow slowly at first and as long as they're sufficiently funded they may achieve steeper growth before maturing and growth slows again.

Venture capitalists understand the 'S' curve very well. They want the steepest growth in the shortest time, with the minimum risk.

So, they buy after the very risky start-up stage – after the company has proved its proposition and then they fund rapid growth and aim to sell before growth tails off.

Once the growth slows at the top of the 'S' curve, it may still be a great business, but it doesn't offer the rapid capital growth that venture capitalists are after.

As growth slows, it's more about maximising profit in order to give shareholders better income in the form of dividends. Mature businesses tend to be selected by investors looking for 'income' rather than 'capital growth'.

This is why mergers and acquisitions are often the best way to achieve growth in a mature market. The merged business can consolidate its cost base, improve its profitability and be better able to protect its increased market share.

Venture Capitalists may be experts in their field, but they know very well how hard it is to get it right. They recognise that the odds of success can be as bad as the following: For every ten businesses they invest in, they may lose money or merely break-even in seven of them, achieve limited growth in two of them and have one success that makes it all worthwhile.

For them it's a numbers game, whereas for you, it may be the only chance of business success you'll ever get. So you have to make sure you get it right.

The need for cash

Doing business can often seem quite complicated, but ultimately it can be summarised into just three parts:

1. Winning it

2. Doing it

3. Getting paid for it.

You need to invest in promoting your products or services to win customers, you need to invest in the infrastructure to provide the products or services and then you often have to wait until the customer is ready to complete the transaction and actually pay you.

So, there's generally a lag between each of these steps and the longer the lag, the more it will add to your trading cash requirement.

If you want to grow you'll need to win more customers and you'll need to increase the infrastructure to service them and hence you'll have a growing cash requirement.

Whether it's creating a website, developing a new product, commissioning a new promotional campaign or taking on a new member or staff – cash has to be outlaid to grow before the resulting growth generates income.

The more rapidly you want to grow your business – the more cash you'll require to support that growth.

Businesses with good profitability still go bust when they try to grow more quickly than their cash reserves can support.

It's cash that counts.

Although profits should eventually translate into cash, it is the immediacy of cash that is critical. The reasons why a business gets into difficulties may vary, but the reason why a business fails is because it runs out of cash.

As a director of a company you have a legal responsibility to cease trading as soon as your business is unable to pay its bills when they fall due.

If you can't get immediate access to additional funding, that's it – it's all over.

And the worst possible time to seek additional funding is when you already have cashflow problems.

When you start a business or grow a business, you need to know whether you will have enough cash to support its growth.

As we explore the various Catch-22s of growing a business and how to overcome them, you'll see the pivotal role played by cash in the heart of business success.

I now want to introduce the various dilemmas and Catch-22s, and to make it easier to see how they all inter-relate with each other we'll link them to the three phases: Entry, Growth and Exit.

The Entry Phase

Let's look at the very beginning of the 'S' curve where businesses are just starting or are currently still small.

A business is extremely vulnerable during the inception stage, because even relatively small impediments can cause a business to fail.

Examples of these impediments might be:

1. A bad debt – even if it's only delayed, it still impacts your cashflow.

2. A system failure – even if your data is backed up, you'll be impeded until it's fixed.

3. A break-in – even if you're insured, you'll be delayed until you replace and reconfigure the stolen computers or equipment.

4. A product failure – you may not have manufactured it, but if you supplied it, you'll still have to deal with it and then seek redress from your supplier. When a customer has ordered multiple items from you and just one of them is faulty, it may give a customer with their own cashflow problems the ideal excuse to delay payment of the whole order.

5. An injury or sickness – if you employ two people and one gets sick you lose a massive 50% of your capacity, if you employ ten people and one gets sick you only lose 10% and of course if you grow to employ one hundred people and one gets sick you only lose a mere 1% of your capacity.

6. A landlord unexpectedly increases your rent – if you're barely making a profit the additional cost may soon become insurmountable. A move to cheaper premises

will cost a large amount in the short-term, perhaps the equivalent of several years of the extra rental charge.

7. A general economic down-turn, as witnessed in 2008 as a result of the so-called 'credit crunch'.

Any of these – and particularly a combination of them – may delay servicing your customers and so delay getting paid, which will impact your cashflow – sometimes catastrophically.

I know of examples for each of these impediments where it has resulted in the failure of a business.

It becomes much easier to understand why the failure rate is so high when you see the impact that relatively minor impediments can have on the viability of a small business.

The impact doesn't only affect cashflow, when customers don't get the service they want at the time they want it they will soon find an alternative supplier.

I've known of several businesses that relied too heavily on just one or two major customers and ended up failing because of that reliance.

Some businesses are actually established knowing that most of their business will come as a result of one or two larger companies.

This can arise because the business owner has contacts with a large company that used to employ them. Or because the employees of a large local company form the majority of the customer base for a small business.

You can see how easily the small business can fail if the large company has to close or decides to move.

If a business doesn't grow beyond its initial vulnerable stage, it isn't so much a question of '*if*' it will fail – it's more a question of '*when*' it will fail.

In order to secure a long-term future a business needs to grow quickly through the vulnerable stage until it has reached a size capable of surviving minor impediments.

But, growth brings its own risks, for example:

- Growth requires more customers meaning more promotional effort

- Extra capacity has to be financed until it can be fully utilised

- Extra capacity has to be supported, which increases overheads

- Extra capacity has to be trained, which impacts existing capacity

- Recruitment mistakes can upset the balance and reduce efficiency.

This is why many small business owners are cautious about committing to the kind of growth required to reach even the first level of stability.

It is often said that the most difficult person for the business owner to employ is the very first one after themselves.

And you can understand why; the first person represents roughly fifty per cent of the company's capability – assuming the business owner is actually contributing to the capacity of the enterprise.

The first employee will have a critical impact on how customers perceive the company and the brand you're trying to build.

The first employee will also have a critical impact on the business owner's view of just about everything.

Get the first one wrong and you may never be inclined to employ a second. They might be indifferent towards your customers, or to you and the business, or regularly turn up late or have many days off sick – yet you're still paying them.

If you embrace growth it means incurring the risks associated with adding capacity, but if you avoid growth you're likely to get hit by the type of impediments that collapse a small business.

I describe this as the Entry Dilemma – when to commit to growth.

The Entry Dilemma – When to grow

It's perilous to stay small <u>and</u> it's hazardous to grow – so when should you aim to grow?

There is a group of people who don't worry about this dilemma. I meet many people who have established themselves as a business, but with absolutely no intention of creating a company for sale or employing anyone else. These people have created employment for themselves and when they retire – their business will retire with them.

This is often a lifestyle choice and is of course perfectly reasonable. The only note of caution is to plan for the mishap of accident or illness that may prevent you from working. You will also need to earn enough to pay into a pension plan and maybe fund insurance in case you can't work for a period.

For these people, success is limited to our first measure because the business <u>is</u> the person. However, this book is aimed at those wishing to grow a business that can exist beyond the creator and at some point be sold.

Most businesses can't even begin trading without a certain level of investment in marketing, infrastructure and people.

The Entry Dilemma is not so much whether to grow, but when to make the first real push for growth.

To give yourself the best chance of success the first real growth push needs to get you all the way to the first Stability Step.

The first Stability Step

The first Stability Step is when a business has reached a level of capacity that can cope with the kind of minor impediments we've discussed <u>and</u> is able to generate a sustainable level of demand that is efficiently matched to that capacity.

In order to have any chance of success a business has to get to the first Stability Step before it gets hit by more impediments than it can cope with. Unfortunately, the rate of business failures indicates that most will lose this race and become just another statistic.

To give your business a chance of long-term success you have to focus on achieving your first Stability Step where you can then take a breather and evaluate how to grow to the next Stability Step.

This means that growth tends not to be a single 'S' curve, but many small versions where the top of each 'S' is a more stable platform that can give some breathing space and preparation time for the next phase of growth.

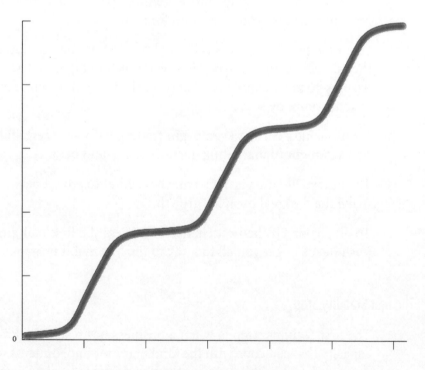

Series of business growth curves

Think of it like climbing a mountain – you move between a succession of stable ledges where you can rest and recuperate or shelter from bad weather. The stages of growth between the stable ledges require you to take some risk, but it's the only way to get to the top.

This means that *growth demands a temporary surrender of security*. With thanks to the author Gail Sheehy, to whom this phrase is first attributed – although she was referring to an individual rather than a business.

I often get asked whether there is a level of turnover that a business needs to reach in order to be stable. The answer is frequently yes, but the level of turnover depends on the type of business.

The Entry Catch-22 – Achieving first base

A Catch-22 is where two actions are mutually dependent on the other action being completed first. Like the person who wants a job but can't get the job without the experience and can only get the experience by having the job.

The Entry Catch-22 refers to the apparent difficulty in getting to the first Stability Step that is essential for further growth and future success. Most banks won't consider a business for even an overdraft until it has survived a year. Yet without that overdraft facility, it may not have the flexibility to get through its first year.

We're now ready to define The Entry Catch-22 – Achieving first base:

To grow to the first Stability Step requires funding – yet funding is only offered to businesses that have already achieved the first Stability Step.

*To grow to the first Stability
Step requires funding*

*Funding is only offered after you've
achieved the first Stability Step*

The beginning of the 'S' curve is a hazardous place that most businesses never get beyond. This is the survival zone, because your chances of survival are statistically poor.

That's why Venture Capitalists only invest in businesses that have already got beyond this phase.

Unless you already have a track record of success, the banks and professional investors don't tend to get involved too early in new ventures. They know that the odds of success are small and the risks to their funding large.

If a bank does agree to lend, it will normally want to secure the loan against the property of the business owner.

The result is that many new ventures are either self-funded or funded by family. Because you or your family are not professional investors, there is a tendency to forego the usual demands for a robust business plan.

Not only is there no route plan to follow, but also there's no advice and support from a professional investor.

So, the poor success rate discourages professional investors from getting involved too early because the risks are too high – yet their failure to get involved early actually contributes to the poor success rate.

Even if you're in the fortunate position of having your own funds to invest in your business, I believe you're more likely to see a return on your investment if you follow the strategies suggested in Part 2 to overcome the Entry Catch-22.

Part 2 of this book deals with how to overcome each of the Catch-22s, but because the Catch-22s all affect each other, I think it's preferable to be introduced to all of them first, so now we'll move onto the next phase.

The Growth Phase

Growth phases are represented in the series of 'S' curves by any of the steep parts.

You can't start a business or begin any new growth phase without the cash reserves to support that growth or access to additional funding.

How rapidly you can grow will depend on your funding. As long as you choose a growth gradient that's matched to your funding capability you should be able to continually fund the trading cashflow and grow.

As mentioned in the Introduction, my work modelling businesses to create business plans has made me very aware of how everything in business seems to depend on everything else and ultimately – everything depends on cash.

Cash gets tied up in premises, machinery, systems, stock, staff and customers.

Usually when you try to minimise the cash required it's at the expense of profit.

If you go for maximising profit it's likely to reduce your available cash for growth or even to survive an impediment.

This is the growth dilemma faced by most business owners.

The Growth Dilemma – When to profit

If you want to grow you need to focus on cash even at the expense of profit, so when should you focus on profit?

Let's look at this dilemma with regard to Capital Expenditure. If you had sufficient cash you could buy equipment outright and get the best possible price, but it would tie up your cash in the equipment so that it can't be used for something else. This is an example of going for profit at the expense of cash.

An alternative would be to lease the equipment and pay for it over a period, it wouldn't tie up so much of your cash, but overall you would pay much more for it. This is an example of going for cash at the expense of profit.

Now let's take a look at buying products from suppliers – it is often possible to get a reduced unit price for a bulk purchase. This may improve your profitability, but it will tie up working capital in excess stock. Another example of going for profit at the expense of cash

Once your cash has been converted into equipment or stock it's no longer available for other purposes. You may appear more profitable, but you may have limited your rate of growth by restricting your available cash. Or you may have even limited your ability to survive.

Despite this, if the cash is available, many small businesses go for profit at the expense of their cash reserves.

In the early stages and in a growth phase, your focus has to be on cash rather than profit. A lack of cash means a lack of growth and more risk for longer.

As growth slows to a stable platform the focus can shift to maximising profit.

Once a business has reached a stable market share, it may be more appropriate to spend extra on stock to maximise profitability and better profitability usually means it will be better able to protect that market share in the face of competition.

We've been discussing the importance of being properly funded if you want your business to grow. If we plot growth in terms of cumulative cash, it tends to have a '*Hockey stick*' profile as shown in the diagram below:

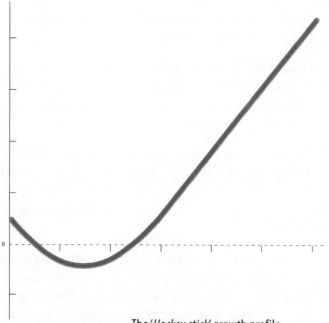

The '*Hockey stick*' growth profile

Cumulative cash is the result of adding the net cash position each month to the month before. So, if you spend more than you receive, as is likely when you start a business or begin a new growth phase, cumulative cash goes down before it goes up.

Hopefully, the results of your growth initiatives will bear fruit and after a time, your cumulative cash will recover and go beyond the position you started from.

When you attempt to grow and your cumulative cash goes down, it doesn't have to go below zero, although in a small business it often does.

An established business may be able to grow by just depleting its cash reserves, whereas a start-up is likely to need access to additional funding.

The most negative point below zero on your cumulative cash graph is what you will need to invest, i.e. your cash requirement. If you can't fund it yourself, you will need to borrow it or find other investment funding.

The steeper you want the angle of the *Hockey stick* shaft to be – i.e. your Growth Gradient – the deeper the negative 'U' is likely to be.

The graph below shows two '*Hockey stick*' profiles indicating that you can have a *steep* shaft only if you're prepared to fund a *deep* 'U'.

Or you can decide to fund a *shallow* 'U' as long as you're prepared to accept a *shallow* shaft.

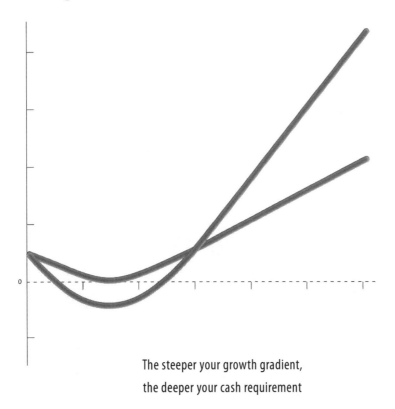

The steeper your growth gradient,

the deeper your cash requirement

If you decide to invest in the deeper 'U' to achieve a steeper growth gradient – you'll be able to reach a specific point quicker, for example your exit point. Remember that our refined definition of success relates to how quickly you achieve that success.

The quicker you want to get to a certain point, the steeper the growth gradient needs to be and the deeper the cash requirement you will need to fund.

So, how much cash do you need? It depends on your desired growth gradient. But what growth gradient should you go for? It depends on your funding capability, which depends on what you will achieve with the investment and how quickly you will achieve it.

The typical problem that arises with small businesses is that they haven't correctly calculated their cash requirement for their desired growth gradient. This may lead them to believe that they can achieve the growth gradient depicted by the hockey stick profile with the steeper shaft, but with only the investment level depicted by the hockey stick profile with the shallow 'U', as shown by the dotted line in the diagram below:

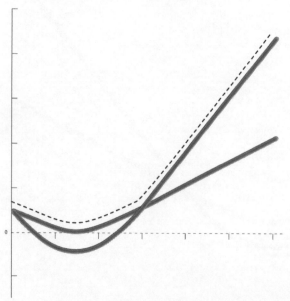

This results in their ambition being out of balance with their funding, which will lead the business into difficulty. And that leads us to the Growth Catch-22 – Balancing growth.

The Growth Catch-22 – Balancing growth

We're now ready to define The Growth Catch-22 – Balancing growth:

Your level of funding dictates your growth gradient and hence your future earnings – yet it is your future earnings that will define the level of funding worth investing.

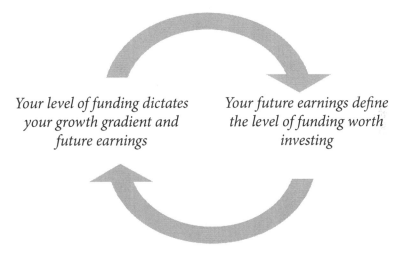

Your level of funding dictates your growth gradient and future earnings

Your future earnings define the level of funding worth investing

So, where should you start?

- With your desired growth gradient defining your funding requirements?

Or

- With your funding limitations dictating your growth gradient?

Will your ambition be free to define your funding or will your funding be allowed to constrain your ambition?

Let's explore the consequences of The Growth Catch-22.

A cashflow problem is actually an *unforeseen* cash requirement. Unforeseen either because you could never have seen it coming or unforeseen because you weren't able to look properly!

If you haven't forecasted your cash requirement, it's more likely to come as a surprise and sometimes as a shock. And then the tendency is to get nervous and throttle back.

The easiest and quickest expenditure to cut is your discretionary spending – usually the very business development activities essential to sustain and grow demand. Discretionary spending might be:

- Promotional activity (growing customers)

- Product development (future customers)

- Recruitment or adding stock (growing capacity)

- Capital expenditure (future capacity).

Cut backs in these areas will at some point result in revenues falling short of targets.

Cash receipts will begin to fall and the funds available for expenditure are further constrained.

If you're lucky, after a while the business will stabilise again rather than go into a spiral of decline.

However, many businesses don't recover and the spiral of decline is terminal. Just like losing your grip on the side of a mountain can be terminal.

If you do manage to stabilise and recover your composure you might make another attempt.

You begin spending again on business development activities. But again there is a delay before the initiatives become cash generators that allow your cumulative cash to recover.

If you didn't correctly calculate the cash requirement, as is common, the extent of cash required will again come as a surprise and you will have a cashflow problem. So again, you fall into the same Catch-22 trap.

This results in the 'Saw-tooth' effect – a growth-decline cycle that approximates to zero growth or *flat lining*.

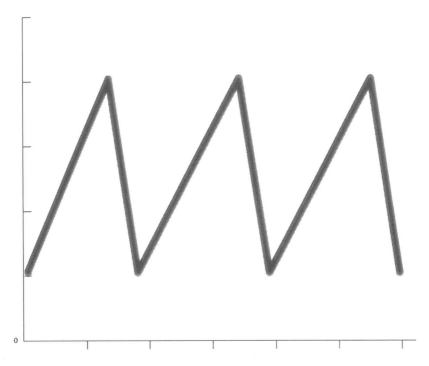

'Saw tooth' profile – like a series of ladders and snakes

The business is expending all the effort, but reaping none of the reward.

I regularly see this effect in companies. In fact, virtually every time I go through this with a small business they nod in agreement, recognising that they've also fallen foul of it.

So, now I begin from the premise that every small business has the propensity to suffer from the Growth Catch-22.

I now run a little experiment on business owners and you can check it out for yourself with a business owner you know.

Strike up a conversation about business generally and then steer it round to the business-owner's company.

Try asking the following two questions:

Question 1:
What is your ambition for your business over the next 3-5 years?

Continue the conversation for a while before asking the second question below so as not to make it too obvious that you will connect the two questions.

Question 2:
What increase are you budgeting for next year?

In my experience the answers to these questions are typically along the following lines:

For question 1, business owners tend to answer ambitiously yet set aside any funding limitations.

The most likely answer to question 1 is strong growth – perhaps a desire to double the turnover within 3 years. This would translate to an annual growth rate of 26%.

For question 2, business owners tend to answer conservatively thinking about funding and risk, yet setting aside any ambition.

The most likely answer to question 2 is modest increases – perhaps around 5 or 10%.

These two answers are clearly out of balance because their medium-term ambition is running at up to five times their short-term expectations.

The problem is that they haven't made a strong connection between their ambition and their ability to fund that ambition.

If this level of discrepancy can occur within the space of a few minutes in the same conversation, it's hardly surprising that it can occur in the midst of all the distractions of running a business.

This is just the kind of imbalance that leads to the *Saw-tooth* effect and stagnation or even decline, but certainly not success.

The *Saw-tooth* profile shows us that running your own business is like a game of *'Snakes and Ladders'*, only you're playing for success or survival of your business and the statistics indicate that the dice is loaded against success.

The problem with small businesses is that their ambition is out of balance with their funding – they have insufficient funding for the desired growth gradient. And it won't be long before they run into trouble and have to throttle back.

They lose their grip on the success mountain and can slip down – even below their previous Stability Step.

They end up spending too much time at the tedious task of managing their cashflow rather than the exciting task of managing their business development and growth initiatives.

This makes the problem even worse and there's every chance they'll stagnate or decline. When a business has cashflow problems, it's not the right time to attract investment.

The Growth Catch-22 refers to the difficulty of finding a balance between ambition and funding. Most small businesses will suffer from the *Saw-tooth* effect at some time. However, if you can overcome this second Catch-22 you have a much better chance of succeeding in the long term.

Imagine if you could take all the ladders of the *Saw-tooth* profile and put them on top of each other without any of the snakes. Instead of *flat lining* – you'd have real growth. You'd be expending all the effort as well as reaping the reward.

This is the aim and to achieve it we have to overcome the Growth Catch-22.

I've already explained that Part 2 of this book deals with how to overcome each of the Catch-22s but now it's time to introduce the third Catch-22. Only then will you understand how they are all interlinked and be equipped to get the most from Part 2.

The Exit Phase

I believe that one of the biggest mistakes made by the owners of small businesses is that they don't consider properly the scalability of the venture and how far they would like to take it.

How much growth might there be in the venture and therefore how much could the business be worth.

Yet this is the main consideration for a professional investor.

For many business owners, the first time they have really considered an exit strategy is when they go to a potential investor for funding and they're forced to confront it.

The investor will want to clearly understand the exit strategy and timescale because that's the point at which the return-on-investment can be properly estimated.

Return-on-investment is the only way that an investor can compare different opportunities and hence is able to make the important decision of *whether* to invest.

Just like the cash we discussed earlier, once the investment is made in a particular venture the funds are no longer available to use for another opportunity in the future.

Even if you don't require an external investor, *you* are investing in your business, but more critically, you're investing your time as well as your money.

It ought to be doubly important for you to carefully consider the return on your time and money. Once you've invested your time and money in an opportunity it's no longer available for an alternative that may have delivered a better return.

I've spoken to many business owners who have not really considered this at all.

When I'm modelling businesses and creating business plans for clients we look at the scalability, likely valuation and potential return of a business; and all too often it's disappointing.

In many cases the business owner should really put their time, talent and money into an alternative venture. But if I propose this course of action the response usually suggests that it's the first time they've ever confronted it; whereas, the serial entrepreneur would be continually considering it.

On the other hand there are businesses that have been owned by the same family for several generations so there are other considerations beyond straight return-on-investment.

There is no right answer; it depends on your circumstances. What I'm suggesting is that you must at least consider it. Then you can make decisions with the necessary knowledge and an understanding of the consequences.

Although we're talking about the Exit Phase, it's really important to spend some time thinking about this right away, to check whether the venture has the potential to meet your expectations.

How much of your working life should you devote to the current business venture and how do you work towards exiting at the best time to maximise the return on your efforts?

This is the Exit Dilemma – When to go.

The Exit Dilemma – When to go

When should you plan to exit to maximise the return on your investment of time and money?

The figure below shows two potential growth gradients for the same venture:

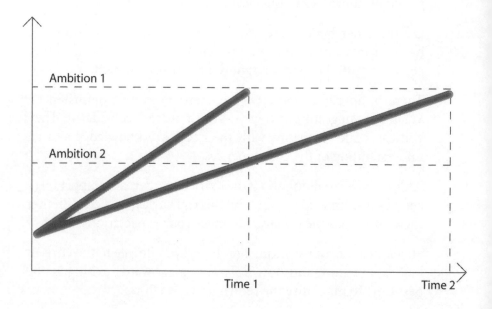

Ambition and time

If you can't or don't want to fund the steep growth gradient that would get you to the higher ambition (Ambition 1) in the shorter time (Time 1), you have a choice:

- Aim for the same exit time (Time 1), but the lower ambition (Ambition 2)

- Aim for the same ambition (Ambition 1), but the longer exit time (Time 2).

Whatever you decide, it will inform your strategy and enable you to plan to succeed to a defined level within a defined timescale and this is essential for success.

Another way to look at it this is to consider how much of your life would you want to dedicate to a particular business. Let's say you have roughly forty years of working life, many people will have already worked for someone else before starting a business, so they may only have thirty or twenty years remaining.

Do you want to spend it all in one business or would you like to have a go at running several?

Choosing an appropriate ambition and timescale is the Exit Dilemma.

We will cover how to work through this dilemma in Part 2, but now we need to cover the Exit Catch-22.

The Exit Catch-22 – Financing ambition

I've referred to the third Catch-22 as the Exit Catch-22 but don't make the mistake of thinking that it's a long way off. I've called it the Exit Catch-22 because that's when the impact really hits you, although the decision to overcome it has to be taken much earlier and often at the very outset.

Hindsight may be a wonderful thing, but even more wonderful is to understand the consequences of your decisions before you take them.

Your exit is likely to be to sell your business in order to invest in a new venture or perhaps retire. So what figure would you like to walk away with?

We're told that we're living longer, so we need an ever-larger pension fund. If you want a similar standard of living to your working years the recommendation is to acquire sufficient funds to deliver two thirds of your salary.

For a business owner this means your fund will need to approach 10 times your final salary to maintain a good standard of living over a reasonable length of retirement. So, if you hope to take £100k from your business each year, you might need your pension fund to approach £1m.

Let's take a look at how the owner of a typical small business might try to achieve this.

Let's suppose that your business has already achieved a level of stability and now has a turnover of £1m.

You decide that you'd like to exit with £1m before tax and because you're the sole shareholder you need to be able to sell the business for £1m.

The type of business will define the likely relationship between turnover, profit and business valuation. We'll assume your business is fairly typical with a ratio of turnover to business valuation of 3:1; meaning that the business is worth a third of its annual turnover.

This means that your business may currently have a nominal valuation of about £333k and that you would need to grow the turnover from £1m to £3m for it to end up with a valuation of £1m.

If you aim to do this within 5 years you would require an annual growth rate of 25%, whereas if you give yourself 10 years your required annual growth rate would reduce to about 12%. Let's suppose you're quite ambitious and want to exit in 5 years.

To achieve 25% annual growth, perhaps you have calculated that you will need to invest £100k of funding, which you don't have, so you decide to find an investor.

As we've suggested, the business currently has a turnover of £1m and the type of business you're in would tend to attract a nominal valuation of a third of the annual turnover.

This means an investor would probably require a 30% share of the business for the £100k invested.

Let's suppose that the £100k invested does indeed produce the desired growth in the five-year timescale and your business now has a valuation of £1m as predicted.

But here's the catch; the investor will receive 30% of the value of the business and you will only receive 70%. So you would have to exit with only £700k instead of the desired £1m.

To get back to £1m you would need to sell the business for £1.4m, which because of the type of business would require a turnover of £4.2m. The growth gradient is now steeper as it needs to grow by £3.2m not by £2m.

This represents an annual growth rate of 33% over 5 years instead of 25%, an increase of 8% growth per year. Many businesses would be happy to achieve a total growth rate of 8%, yet you need it as extra growth just to compensate for the investment.

To achieve the new level of growth in the same timescale would require a greater level of funding and, of course, the investor will want an even larger share of the business at the outset.

But then, of course, the amount you receive on exit will be reduced again and you will need to grow even faster to compensate.

You end up in a circular predicament that I've called the Exit Catch-22.

Let's define The Exit Catch-22 – Financing ambition:

Your desired exit valuation requires a level of funding – yet the level of funding increases the exit valuation you require.

Your desired exit valuation requires a level of funding   *The level of funding increases the exit valuation you require*

You can now see why the solution to the problem has to be thought about beforehand.

It's easy to understand The Exit Catch-22 when it relates to a new investor who is funding your growth in return for a share of the business. However, it also applies if you opt for a loan to fund your growth.

Let's suppose that you ask your bank for a loan over 5 years. The cash requirement is your most negative cumulative cash position, and as soon as you take out a loan you have to fund the loan repayments and pay monthly interest on the outstanding balance of the loan. Month by month these accumulate to give you a deeper cumulative cash requirement.

The loan has to cover your worse case requirement; but each month the loan is adding to this cumulative requirement, therefore you need much more than the original estimate of your cash requirement simply to service the debt.

So, you re-calculate with a larger loan and the same thing happens.

When you finally get to a balanced position the size of the loan is much larger than you would have imagined. Try it for yourself.

What happens if you don't bother to recalculate or decide you can manage on a smaller loan and you only borrow the original value? If you still attempt the original growth gradient, you are likely to run into cashflow problems.

Banks get very nervous if you go back after a few months and tell them that you got it wrong and you actually should have asked for more. In many cases the bank may have lent more if you'd originally requested it, but asking for it subsequently will often meet with rejection because they've lost confidence in you as a business manager.

Banks will only lend if they are confident that you will use the funds to generate future income that will enable you to service the debt, i.e. pay it back with interest. After all, that's their business model.

A new investor will also want to be sure their cash is going towards driving growth – not bailing out existing obligations.

So, now you're under-funded and you're back to managing your cashflow again; only this time you've got a debt to service as well. You end up turning off your discretionary spending and again you fall foul of the *Saw-tooth* effect discussed in the Growth Catch-22. Which means that you will have put in all the effort yet reaped none of the reward.

The banks are also likely to want security, usually against property and you may not have sufficient for the size of the loan. This is why many business owners prefer the option of finding an investor without realising the extent of the Exit Catch-22.

Of course, without investment you won't be able to grow. So you might want to apply the argument that 70% of a decent business valuation is better than 100% of a paltry valuation. The point is that you should always be aware of the Exit Catch-22 so that you can make the best decisions.

So, that's it, we've covered the Dilemmas and Catch-22s applicable to Entry, Growth and Exit and only by understanding and dealing with each one are you likely to be successful.

It's no wonder the odds of a business surviving are so small, never mind achieving any worthwhile level of success.

So, are you mad to set yourself up in business, or is there a way to make the best decisions for each of the dilemmas and break into the circularity of each of the Catch-22s to overcome them and achieve success?

The first part of overcoming *any* problem is to recognise and understand it and that's been the objective of the first part of this book.

The second part of this book introduces the heart of business success to help you decide how to make your dilemma decisions and overcome the Catch-22s of growing a business. Only then will you stand a chance of busting the appalling odds and becoming one of the elite few to succeed.

The third part of this book suggests how you can incorporate this knowledge into planning your success.

Just before we move onto Part 2, let's summarise what we've covered so far.

Summary of Part 1

There is a Dilemma and a Catch-22 for each of the three phases of business Entry, Growth and Exit that collectively conspire against an enthusiastic entrepreneur and contribute to the appalling statistics on business failure rates.

Although they are introduced within separate phases they all have a tendency to be inter-dependent – connected to each other – and you need to consider them collectively to be successful.

Entry Phase

If you stay at the bottom of the 'S' curve you're at risk from relatively small impediments and it's only a matter of time before you get hit by one. So you have to grow to survive, but growth itself is hazardous and growth requires investment.

Whether to grow and when to grow is the Entry Dilemma facing start-ups and small businesses. You have to grow quickly to the first Stability Step, where you can operate with more efficiency and profitability, which will enable you to survive minor impediments. Yet how do you grow to the first Stability Step when nobody is prepared to invest until you've already got there? This is the Entry Catch-22.

Growth Phase

It's often better value to buy in bulk or pay for capital equipment in a single lump sum, but this uses up your available cash so that it's no longer available to help you grow or avoid impediments. This is the Growth Dilemma

Growth for many businesses is a succession of ladders and snakes producing a *Saw-tooth* profile where you're expending all the effort but reaping none of the reward.

This occurs because the lag between investment in business development initiatives and the cash receipts resulting from those initiatives creates a cash requirement that is often bigger than anticipated.

If you haven't correctly estimated the impact of growth on your cashflow it will be a surprise to you. If it comes as a surprise, you may not have sufficient cash to fund it and you're likely to experience a cashflow problem causing you to throttle back and possibly leading to the *saw-tooth* profile.

Profitable companies can still go bust if they try to grow more quickly than their cash reserves will allow – it's cash that counts.

What it's worth investing depends on the likely returns, but the likely returns depend on what you invest. Getting this balance right is the Growth Catch-22.

Exit Phase

How much of your working life should you devote to the current business venture and how do you work towards exiting at the best time to maximise the return on your efforts? This is the Exit Dilemma.

If you obtain external funding to help you grow, a significant proportion is immediately absorbed servicing that funding, so you actually need more. The impact of this Catch-22 only occurs on exit and hence this is referred to as the Exit Catch-22.

Summary of Dilemmas and Catch-22s

The Entry Dilemma – When to grow

It's perilous to stay small <u>and</u> it's hazardous to grow – so when should you aim to grow?

The Growth Dilemma – When to profit

If you want to grow you need to focus on cash even at the expense of profit, so when should you focus on profit?

The Exit Dilemma – When to go

When should you plan to exit to maximise the return on your investment of time and money?

The Entry Catch-22 – Achieving first base:

To grow to the first Stability Step requires funding – yet funding is only offered to businesses that have already achieved the first Stability Step.

The Growth Catch-22 – Balancing growth:

Your level of funding dictates your growth gradient and hence your future earnings – yet it is your future earnings that will define the level of funding worth investing.

The Exit Catch-22 – Financing ambition:

Your desired exit valuation requires a level of funding – yet the level of funding increases the exit valuation you require.

Summary Table	Dilemma	Catch-22
Entry Phase	When to grow	Achieving first base
Growth Phases	When to profit	Balancing growth
Exit Phase	When to go	Financing ambition

Part Two

Overcoming the Catch-22s

As mentioned in the Introduction, published statistics tell us that the odds of a new business succeeding are shockingly bad.

In Part 1, we discussed what success might mean and introduced the Dilemmas and Catch-22s that conspire against success.

Now we're going to introduce the heart of business success and show how it can be used as a basis for making your dilemma decisions and overcoming the various Catch-22s to ensure you're one of the elite few to succeed.

The heart of business success

We've already discussed how cash has a pivotal role in business failures or in your ability to succeed. We also discussed how customers and capacity have to be in balance to achieve efficiency and stability.

Business success is related to keeping these three critical 'C's: Customers, Capacity and Cash in balance as you grow.

Customers, Capacity and Cash are the key elements of the heart model as shown in the following illustration:

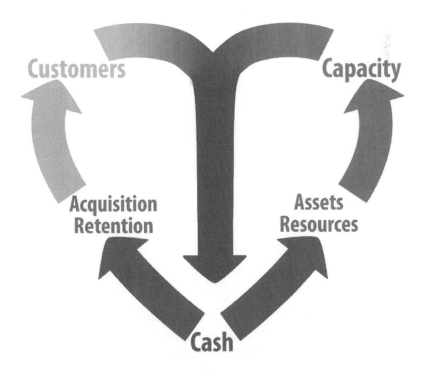

The heart of business success

For a business to be successful it must pump cash into Acquiring and Retaining customers; it must also pump cash into developing its Assets and Resources to deliver sufficient capacity to service its growing customer numbers.

I've chosen to refer to this as the 'heart of business success', firstly because the heart is a pump that we're all familiar with – and we know what happens to us if it gets out of rhythm – and secondly because if you get the balance right it really is the heart of your business success.

We know that when we are feeling healthy we can be more energetic, enthusiastic and enjoy life – the same effect occurs when our business is healthy and in balance.

Regardless of the type of business, it can be modelled using the three critical 'C's, Customers, Capacity and Cash and the relationship between them.

Cash

Cash is the critical life-blood of a business. By law a business must cease to trade if it doesn't have sufficient funds to pay its bills when they fall due. Therefore, Cash in our heart diagram is coloured in 'mission critical' red and I've placed it in the foundation position. This is the fulcrum or balance point about which the whole heart can topple if it gets out of balance.

Capacity

Capacity is coloured blue in our heart diagram as the greater your Assets and Resources the more 'blue chip' the company will be perceived to be.

Assets have to be paid for and usually appear on the company's balance sheet; these can be both tangible assets, such as property and machinery as well as intangible assets such as trademarks and patents.

Resources require cash but are not owned and will not appear on the balance sheet; the most obvious example is the expertise of your management team and employees.

Customers

Customers are coloured yellow in our heart diagram because yellow indicates the transient nature of customers. They are 'fickle' and if they're dissatisfied they will defect to the competition.

The acquisition of new customers usually requires some form of promotional activity which has to be funded.

If your existing customers are well-served they will be more satisfied and be retained for longer. The better your customer retention the fewer new customers you will need to acquire to achieve the same growth gradient.

Maintaining Balance

If Customers and Capacity are in balance the two primary colours of yellow and blue representing them will produce green and our heart diagram shows the resulting 'Cash-in' for the business as green.

If you spend more cash on your capacity and on winning customers than you earn from customers the red will outweigh your green and you will need access to funding or go out of business.

If your capacity gets too heavy in relation to your customer demand, the heart will topple out of balance towards capacity and you will be burning your cash reserves.

But you also don't want your customers to be served only satisfactorily – you want them to be served well enough to tell everyone about your great service.

So, if your customers get too heavy in relation to your capacity to service them, the heart will topple out of balance towards customers. But if this means your service levels begin to deteriorate it won't be long before your customers will start to defect to the competition. The rate of defection may be hard to stem and it may swing back into balance briefly and continue right through the balance point and over the other way towards capacity.

To achieve a healthy business, you should aim to keep the heart of business success in balance as your business grows.

Priming the pump

To stimulate growth, the pump has to be primed by the injection of cash into the business. This is required to start a business or to launch every new growth phase.

The type of business will affect whether the pump is primed to drive customers and then add capacity to match or primed to drive capacity and then acquire customers to match.

Capacity-driven businesses

Businesses that are primarily driven by capacity will be constrained by resources, for example: the number of restaurant covers, the number of treatment rooms or the number of trained experts or the capacity of production lines or stocking levels.

Promotional activity is then designed to drive sufficient customer numbers to match capacity. Growth usually requires investment in chunks, for each new unit of additional capacity e.g. an extra employee, an extra outlet, an extra production line.

Types of businesses that are primarily capacity-driven include: restaurant, children's nursery, beauty salon, therapy centre e.g. physiotherapy and any service-based business especially those that require a high level of expertise.

This category also includes product-based businesses that have to build or purchase in batches.

Customer driven businesses

Businesses that are primarily driven by customer numbers might be constrained by the market share that can reasonably be achieved given the competition, but they are unlikely to be constrained by capacity limitations.

Capacity can be scaled to match the success of customer acquisition.

The constraint is related to customers, i.e. the size of the market. If the catchment area of such a business is restricted to a certain size, the market for its services is also restricted and when the competition is taken into account there is likely to be a limit to the market share that it is realistic to target.

Up to this point, you just keep adding capacity as you grow.

Types of businesses that are customer-driven include: most Internet businesses, trading companies that can purchase products on the open market, any service-based business where capacity can be outsourced or recruited from a general pool.

This category also includes product-based businesses that are able to build or purchase in small batches or to customer order.

Understanding the inter-dependence between Customers, Capacity and Cash for your business is critical to successfully growing it.

We're now going to discuss each business phase and how to apply the heart model to overcome the Dilemma and Catch-22 associated with that phase.

The Entry Phase

The Entry Dilemma is deciding when to push for growth.

The Entry Catch-22 relates to funding your entry growth phase and is defined as follows:

To grow to the first Stability Step requires funding – yet funding is only offered to businesses that have already achieved the first Stability Step.

Reaching the first Stability Step means your business is no longer in the survival zone, where even small impediments and particularly a combination of impediments can force you out of business. Remember, most businesses won't get to the first Stability Step.

Even if you don't require access to external funds to get your business to the first Stability Step, I strongly recommend you follow the strategies suggested to overcome this Catch-22.

In order to investigate the options for overcoming this Catch-22 we first need to explore what I mean by the first Stability Step in more detail.

The heart of business success shows us that stability requires a good match between Customers and Capacity in order to remain in balance.

Balancing Customers and Capacity

Managing growth is often about deciding when to add capacity and how to minimise cash lost due to under-utilisation or over-capacity:

- For a service-based business under-utilisation may occur when you add an extra employee to your capacity

- For a product-based business over-capacity may occur when you add a new batch of stock to your capacity.

Under-utilisation or over-capacity temporarily tips the heart of business success out of balance towards the capacity side until you can increase your customer numbers to match.

Obviously, you would want to limit the amount of under-utilisation as it ties up your working capital for no sales benefit.

During a period of excess capacity your cash is being depleted, which makes you less able to withstand an impediment.

You would naturally tend to hold off adding to your capacity until your sales pipeline is able to deliver sufficient demand.

But in the early stages of a business, it is all too easy to run into problems due to lack of capacity such that customers may be inconvenienced:

- For a service-based business, customers may be inconvenienced when you have periods of absence

- For a product-based business customers may be inconvenienced when you have supply problems and stock-outs.

Lack of capacity temporarily tips the heart model out of balance towards the customer side. This may represent lost opportunity and lost income, but even worse is the dissatisfaction it is likely to cause your customers.

The better you can maintain a good balance between customers and capacity the greater the efficiency of your business and the opportunity for growth.

Unfortunately, whenever you add capacity, you are likely to create an imbalance – even if only temporarily.

Under-utilisation or over-capacity is depicted in the figure below:

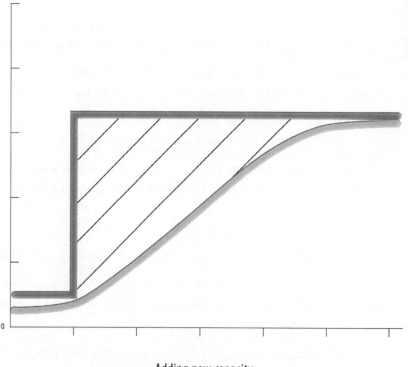

Adding new capacity

The addition of new capacity is shown as a sudden jump and the sloping line depicts the acquisition of new customer demand. The shaded area between the two lines indicates the under-utilisation or over-capacity.

Every time you add a chunk of new capacity, you not only have to fund this capacity immediately, you should also plan to fund promotional activity to deliver the growth in customer demand to match the new level of capacity.

There is always a delay between promotional activity and the results in terms of customer orders; getting the timing right to minimise under-utilisation and over-capacity is a difficult task.

It certainly isn't likely that an exact match can be achieved, but you should aim to do better than our earlier graph and plan for a steeper rise in customers to match the new capacity as depicted in the alternative graph shown below:

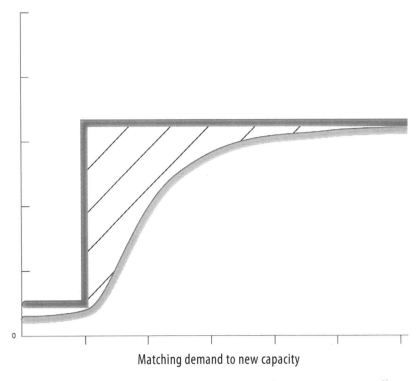

Matching demand to new capacity

For many businesses the issue of matching demand to new capacity is not as straightforward as illustrated in the above sketches. It is nearly always necessary to have more than one type of resource in order to service your customers.

It often makes no sense to grow by adding a single person because it doesn't take you to the next Stability Step. It's better to add nobody for a longer period, build up your cash reserves and then grow by adding sufficient capacity to reach the next point of efficiency and run more promotional activity to drive additional demand.

As a business grows it would normally have to take on the different resource types at different rates.

Let's look at a couple of examples:

- A printing company may typically need 1 finisher for every 2 minders

- An engineering firm may need 1 test engineer for every 3 engineers

- A plumbing company may need 1 CORGI registered gas plumber for every 4 general plumbers

- An Accountancy practice may find that every partner can manage 5 accountants and each accountant is supported by 2 book keepers.

Let's take a simple example of a business where, to service a typical customer it takes 2 hours of Type 'A' resource for every hour of Type 'B' resource. Now let's consider the first point of efficiency and then the first Stability Step.

The first point of efficiency

In our example, the first point of efficiency occurs when the business has 2 Type 'A' resources and 1 Type 'B' resource. The two resource types are perfectly matched and potentially there is no under-utilisation of either resource.

Although this may be the first point of efficiency and all required resource types are matched, it is not a Stability Step; because if resource 'B' is absent, you will have a bottleneck that prevents you servicing customers and delays the receipt of cash.

The first Stability Step

The first Stability Step can only occur when we have at least 2 of each resource type to allow for absences. In our example we would require 4 'A' resources to match our 2 'B' resources; giving a total of 6.

Depending on the type of work undertaken, it might make good economic sense to pay for training to enable some of your 'A' resources to be qualified to cover for your 'B' resources. But this may be inappropriate for some types of work.

This will only be a Stability Step if the business is able to continually attract sufficient customer demand for this level of capacity.

So, the first Stability Step occurs when a business has capacity with no bottlenecks due to absence <u>and</u> sufficient customer demand to keep them all well-utilised.

The business should then be at a point of efficiency and hence profitability, which will enable it to prepare itself well for its next assent. In between such points, during periods of growth, a business is likely to be less efficient, less profitable and less stable because it is harder to closely match demand and capacity.

But how many start-up businesses would go straight to a Stability Step? Most will add capacity incrementally one person at a time. This puts them at risk for longer.

The 'big bang' approach to achieving the first Stability Step

Ideally, we want a start-up business to begin trading immediately at the first Stability Step in what I like to refer to as a 'Big Bang' solution.

This has to be the best way to win the race to stability before the impediments trip you up. But how realistic is it?

Consider a business that has no choice but to start with a 'big bang' approach – like a restaurant.

A restaurant owner can't pay rent and rates only on the tables that are occupied – all the capacity has to be paid for from the outset, regardless of whether there are any customers sitting at the tables.

A restaurant business reaches a Stability Step when it has sufficient occupancy on enough days of the week to be able to not only make a profit, but also to employ enough catering staff to cope with unexpected absences without inconveniencing customers.

A restaurant business perfectly illustrates the necessity to apply the 'big bang' approach because actually – it has no other option. At least as far as the capacity side of the equation is concerned, yet bizarrely, restaurant owners frequently fail to adopt the 'big bang' approach to customer acquisition.

How many times do you see new restaurants open with very few customers? And if you were browsing for somewhere to eat would you then pass it by in favour of a restaurant more fully occupied? Most people believe that if a restaurant is any good it will have people choosing to eat there.

The problem is that the restaurant owner may have spent all the investment capital on refurbishing the restaurant and getting the capacity just right that there's not enough left to properly market the business and attract customers in sufficient numbers. This applies to investment of both time and money.

Perhaps they're under the misconception that supply creates its own demand.

This assumption may hold some truth when you're the only ticket in town – but these days there's over-supply in almost every market and for most places that includes restaurants.

So, the restaurant owner who has no choice but to open with a 'big bang' as far as capacity is concerned, but has not opened with a 'big bang' on the customer side of the business has a problem. Customers and capacity are out of balance, there is massive under-utilisation and the business will be haemorrhaging cash at a terrifying rate.

The heart model indicates that customers and capacity must be in balance for a successful cash outcome. So in our restaurant example the owner and any backers will, at the very least, be feeling the palpitations of that imbalance.

To start immediately at a Stability Step the restaurant owner should plan a marketing campaign to ensure the restaurant can approach capacity from the day it opens. This requires a promotional strategy that doesn't blow itself out immediately after the initial excitement of the launch day – and goes on delivering customers day after day. We'll discuss the promotional aspect of passing trade or 'footfall' later in the book.

It's not just a restaurant business that has to apply the 'big bang' approach in order to be successful – any business that must open with a big chunk of capacity rather than add it incrementally is in the same position.

This may include a product-based business that can only buy stock in large batches. It will have to invest in the whole batch before it can sell a single item off the shelf. Of course, if customers are prepared to wait, you could pre-sell before committing, but if your potential customers can get it off-the-shelf somewhere else, they would need a very persuasive incentive to entice them to wait.

Businesses that have no choice but to open with a big chunk of capacity illustrate how the 'big bang' approach can work if properly planned and fully funded.

Now, I'd like to suggest that it isn't just those with no choice, but every business that wants to succeed and especially if they want to succeed quickly, should adopt the 'big bang' strategy.

The heart model helps us to understand that points of stability occur when a business has reached a level of capacity that can cope with minor impediments without inconveniencing customers and is able to generate a sustainable level of demand that is efficiently-matched to this capacity.

But will you have the courage of your conviction to adopt the 'big bang' approach and give your business a fighting chance of succeeding?

Is the 'big bang' approach right for you?

There's a huge amount of planning and preparation required in order to achieve the 'big bang' approach, but it would give a new business an amazing start on its road to success.

Unfortunately, there are usually two other hurdles to overcome:

1. Belief in yourself and your venture

2. Funding.

The first of these relates to the Entry Dilemma and when you *believe* that you're ready to go for it is probably when you *are* ready to go for it.

The second relates to funding and is the Entry Catch-22 and we'll come back to overcoming the entry Catch-22 in a moment; but first let's cover point 1 and your self-belief and conviction.

Time to burn the boats

The word Strategy comes from the Greek word 'Strategos', meaning 'Army Leader' or 'General'. The Greek army leaders had an interesting strategy when it came to engendering unfailing commitment from their warriors – they removed the option to retreat. When they landed on their enemy's territory, the first order given by the General was to 'burn the boats'.

It's what Alexander the Great did when his army moved on Asia.

When there's no turning back and you have to succeed or die trying, the level of commitment can compensate for a whole host of other inadequacies including being significantly out-numbered or out-gunned.

Unlike the Greek warriors, I hope you're not literally going to die trying, but when you focus on the main activity and leave alone all the safety net options that you keep tinkering with just in case – it's the same as burning the boats.

The reason I want to include this here is because of the dramatic effect your commitment can have on the people whose help you'll need to ensure your success. And it's amazing how this can reduce the cash required to reach the first Stability Step, which is why it needs to be covered first.

To succeed, a business has to grow. But when a company tries to grow, there's always a significant risk of failure. And most people have an inbuilt fear of failure.

Successful entrepreneurs have been shown to have a much healthier attitude to failure. They see it as a learning opportunity and get straight back on their feet and try again. They treat failure as delay rather than defeat and have the confidence to know that eventually they will succeed.

A great example of this is the tenacity shown by the inventor Thomas Edison (1847 – 1931) when testing different configurations of the light bulb. He needed to test thousands of different combinations to find one that would be reliable enough to be commercially viable.

Faced with so many failed attempts, people wondered why he didn't just give up and Edison is quoted as saying: *"I haven't failed. I've just found ten thousand ways that won't work."*

Over his career, Edison amassed over one thousand patents and his incredible success eventually became the global giant General Electric Company (GEC).

Edison is a perfect example of what the British politician Sir Winston Churchill (1874 – 1965) was referring to when he suggested that *"success is the ability to go from one failure to another with no loss of enthusiasm"*.

This refers to the recognition that the route to success is rarely smooth and those that succeed have the ability to keep going with their enthusiasm intact.

Unfortunately, for most people the fear of failure seems to be a major barrier to taking positive action. Ironically, this fear actually secures the failure they're so keen to avoid.

If you genuinely have the confidence of your conviction you're much more likely to present an aura of success. People are naturally attracted to those they believe will succeed and naturally walk away from anyone who presents themselves with insufficient confidence.

I'm not suggesting you should be overly confident or even arrogant – you just need to really believe in yourself and you're ability to succeed.

Next time you go to a networking event try standing at the edge and observing the interaction between people and see if you can identify those that tend to attract and those that tend to repel.

Let's see how important this can be for your business by considering some of the people from whom you may need to seek support. These may include investors, suppliers and anyone considering whether to work with you – especially if their reputation may be affected or if they're prepared to work initially below the market rate and sometimes even for nothing.

Banks and Investors

Banks and investors will of course want to read your business plan, but if they're interested they will want to scrutinise your understanding of the issues and the level of your self-belief and commitment.

Lenders and investors don't invest in a business plan they invest in the people behind the plan – the people who will implement it and ensure its viability.

Investors will tell you that if they have the choice between a strong proposition with an average attitude and a weak proposition with a strong attitude they'll side with the attitude every time.

It's also why banks and investors will want you to put your own cash or even your house on the line for your business before they'll provide any of their cash. They want to be sure that you're fully committed and really believe you can make it a success.

Suppliers

Credit terms from your suppliers can have a significant impact on your cashflow.

The more you outsource, the more significant your suppliers will become to your success. It takes some effort for a supplier to take on a new customer and some risk to take on a new venture if you want them to provide credit terms.

They will check your credit rating, but they may be prepared to take a chance even against a poor rating on the basis that if you succeed, you could become a significant customer in the future.

So, they will need to believe that you have the necessary capability and the commitment to succeed

Even if they don't extend credit initially, you can keep trying as your trading history and continued relationship get stronger.

Partners

A partner is any person or company that works with you to achieve your goals. This may or may not mean that a fee is charged, it could simply be a reciprocal arrangement whereby you aim to help each other by referring potential customers.

If they're going to align themselves with you and particularly their brand with yours, they will need to believe in you and your ability to deliver.

Public Relations (PR)

PR can be a great way to promote your business, but if you want free PR the person responsible for editorial content will again need to believe in you.

It can be a win-win situation where you get the benefit of coverage and promotion of your business and they benefit from filling their content by the deadline.

PR may be general content about you or your business but more commonly refers to a specific event.

If you become known as an expert in your field you can gain PR in the form of interviews or comments when there's a topical news item relating to your area of expertise.

PR may occur in a printed publication or via the Internet or on radio or even on television.

Whatever it is, the person responsible will have to feel they can trust and believe in you. They will be happy to promote you if they already believe that you're successful.

If they perceive that you're relying on this PR to help make you successful, they'll be more reluctant to risk their reputation. There's always plenty of opportunity to fill content without them having to take any risks.

The more you present success the more chance you will have that others will help you deliver that success.

The American historian and social critic Christopher (Kit) Lasch (1932 – 1994) suggested that: *"Nothing succeeds like the appearance of success."*

Business is conducted between people

Business is conducted between people and when people recommend you to others, perhaps as a supplier or as a potential partner, they need to know that their own reputation won't be tarnished as a result. They have to be confident that you will perform to the level you said you would.

The way this tends to work depends on how brightly your commitment to success shines through and on how confident they are with your commitment to perform:

- Your commitment to success does not shine brightly – you'll have to prove yourself by your actions before they'll believe in you sufficiently to give you support. This takes time and is likely to slow your progress.

- Your commitment shines brightly – they're more likely to offer immediate trust. Of course if you let them down, you'll probably never get a second chance and they may even speak negatively about you to others.

Make sure you only say that you'll do something if you really intend to do it. And if you're not sure you'll be able to do something, it is better not to mention it until you've done it. That way, you'll always over-deliver against expectations.

I have a client who has developed a new proposition with no precedent in the market. This means there was little to help people grasp the concept, the business or the opportunity. This kind of challenge requires somebody to champion it with passion and belief.

My client is just such a person and believes totally in his business and in a successful outcome and he presents himself confidently and assertively without arrogance. The result is that people are prepared to connect him to others in their network willingly and quickly.

He has been able to attract editorial coverage in the UK's top national newspapers, which is a great form of free promotion.

Well-connected people have offered their services initially for no fee taking payment only on results.

Sure my client has had to work very hard and he's had some setbacks, but he learns from them and moves on.

The main point I want to get across is that my client's attitude is infectious to those who work closely with him or come into contact with him.

Everything happens quickly for this person because he naturally presents a 'can do' attitude and an aura of success.

Some younger people I meet are concerned that their relatively young age is a barrier to being taken seriously. I sometimes wonder whether the barrier is more of their own making than their audience. The client I just mentioned is relatively young, but his positive attitude would never allow age to present a barrier.

If you talk with authority, that's what they'll afford you, whether you're talking one-to-one or one-to-many.

Your own self-belief and commitment to success is important so you can get others to help you achieve your goals more quickly. And speed is important because to succeed in business you have to be generating sufficient revenues before the cash runs out.

Babbage versus Gates

There is an urgency to promote to customers that have a need for your product or service as soon as possible – before the cash runs out or so that the amount of cash required is not so large in the first place.

Your commitment has to be to the success of the business as a whole and not just to the technical success of your product or of building up your capacity without building customer demand to match.

You only have to reflect on the number of times an inferior product has succeeded against a more technically competent rival because of the attitude to get customers rather than keep refining the product.

Let's take a moment to reflect on the importance of this issue by considering two key figures in the world of computers, Charles Babbage and Bill Gates.

Charles Babbage (1791 – 1871) was a nineteenth century engineer known to some as the 'Father of computing' because he designed and built prototypes of a mechanical computer, which he called a Difference Engine and later enhanced and called an Analytical Machine.

Charles Babbage may have been a genius as an engineer, but he failed to grasp the fundamental consequence of never bringing a product to market.

Charles Babbage was continually striving to make the product as advanced as he could. His initial design was for six decimal places and a second-order difference; but he began planning for 20 decimal places and a sixth-order difference.

B.V. Bowden suggested of Babbage that *"His ambition to build immediately the largest Difference Engine that could ever be needed probably delayed the exploitation of his own ideas for a century"*.

Babbage had received grants from the UK Government, but continually sought more funds for his improved designs. Eventually, Prime Minister Robert Peel recommended that *"Babbage's machine be set to calculate the time at which it would be of use"*.

To achieve perfection may be generally considered a good thing, but we have to resist the temptation to keep doing so when it could already be generating sales.

Not only will the sales of a product be able to contribute to funding its own development, but also the feedback received from customers using it in real situations will be invaluable in highlighting how it should be developed.

By contrast, Bill Gates (born 1955), founder of the hugely successful Microsoft Corporation has always understood the importance of getting products to market and gaining feedback from customers.

His approach to business is illustrated by the way Microsoft came into being.

It has been widely reported that in 1975 Bill Gates believed that he and his colleague, Paul Allen, could build a BASIC interpreter for a new microcomputer recently launched. He contacted the manufacturers and asked them if they would be interested. The company was indeed interested and asked for a demonstration as soon as possible.

Within the next few weeks they had to work speedily to develop a prototype.

The demonstration was a success and in 1976 Microsoft was born. It went on to become the dominant global software giant we know today and made Bill Gates a personal fortune that places him towards the top of the global rich list.

The contrast between Charles Babbage and Bill Gates is striking and the lesson to learn is the importance of knowing what customers need or want and developing and marketing your solutions ahead of the competition.

In 2000 Bill Gates relinquished his position as Chief Executive Officer of Microsoft although he remains Chairman, to concentrate on his charitable foundation. His foundation aims to overcome some of the global problems that Governments and other organisations have struggled to deal with, such as the ambition to eradicate malaria in Africa. He's using his success to find significance through philanthropy.

Attitude and the restaurant example

Let's consider attitude and commitment in the restaurant example. I've seen several restaurants open on side roads, off the High Street and I've asked the owners why they chose the location.

The answer was always the same, simply because the rent was that much lower.

There's a good reason for the rent being lower; it's because the passing trade commonly referred to as 'footfall' is lower. The market rate the landlord can charge is usually related to the size of the premises and the 'footfall'.

The costs of the refurbishment of the premises and establishing the capacity to service customers will be the same whether the restaurant is on a side street or the High Street.

The difference in rent and rates only really comes into effect once the restaurant is trading.

There may be a couple of months during the refurbishment when you would have to budget more for the rent and rates of a High Street location when you still don't have the ability to trade, but that's a relatively small cost.

The higher rent is only a problem if you don't have sufficient customers.

So, I would suggest it comes down to the attitude of the business owner.

Those that go for the side street haven't quite burnt their boats and gone for it. They're trying to go for the cheaper option because they don't have the conviction to really go for success. And as mentioned earlier, this lack of conviction is likely to result in the failure they're so keen to avoid.

Like me, you will have seen restaurants open on a side street, seen them struggle and seen them close.

It's much better to go for the 'big bang' approach to customer acquisition and that's a lot easier on the High Street with the higher 'footfall'.

If you go for the side street and have a lower 'footfall' you'll have to spend more cash generating custom through other promotional initiatives. Not only will you have to spend the cash, you'll also have to spend the time creating and managing those initiatives.

Restaurants that select a side street tend to have to work much harder on quality, service and value for money to get repeat business and much harder on marketing to get the customers there in the first place. This is likely to be even worse in an economic downturn.

Going for the High Street means more people just passing your window and getting to see the ambience you've created and the menu on offer.

I recommend that the difference in rent between the side street and the High Street be thought of as part of the promotional budget. The cost is still in your overheads, but it creates a clearer link to the benefit of the cash outlaid on extra rent each month.

Those that go for the High Street location are aiming for success. They understand that if you want to run a popular restaurant, you should open it in a place where it's popular to eat.

Deciding when to grow

Attitude and commitment are essential for your success and only when you have strong attitude and commitment will you be ready to go for growth.

Without the right attitude and self-belief you will inevitably add to the statistics for business failures.

In my experience the best way to boost your confidence in your business or business idea is to create a well-considered business plan that you truly believe you can deliver. This is covered in more detail in Part 3 of this book.

A well-structured business plan helps you to work through your options and reject those options that are unlikely to deliver your ambition. It will also help you to fully embrace those that are likely to produce the results you need.

It requires you to work out the cash requirement for the level of success you desire and how you will fund it.

We haven't covered all of this yet, because we can't deal with it all at the same time and as we've already come to understand – everything in business depends on everything else.

When you see the future of your business properly planned with details of how you will overcome the various Catch-22s, you will start to really believe that it is possible.

This will give you the boost you need to confidently make it happen.

When you have that confidence, you're more likely to project an aura of success and this will help you get things done more quickly and often for a lot less cash.

When you have the plan completed and you have the desire and the conviction to pull it off, that's when you should go for it.

Clear your mind of distractions and focus, focus, focus on running as hard as you can for the first Stability Step before you get hit by one or more impediments.

Overcoming the Entry Catch-22

We've been discussing the two hurdles that prevent you getting to the first Stability Step via the 'big bang' approach:

1. Belief in yourself and your venture

2. Funding.

We've just dealt with the first of these and when you *believe* that you're ready to go for it – that's probably when you *are* ready to go for it.

So, now let's move onto the issue of the funding required to get to the first Stability Step, the Entry Catch-22.

The Entry Catch-22 is defined as follows:

To grow to the first Stability Step requires funding – yet loans or investment are only offered to businesses that have already achieved stability

To grow to the first Stability Step   *Funding is only offered after you've*
requires funding   *achieved the first Stability Step*

You want to minimise the chances of failure in the early stages, so regardless of the type of business, ideally you need a 'big bang' approach and a go-for-it attitude to get you quickly to the first Stability Step.

The heart model reminds us that cash is required for marketing to deliver customer demand at the same time as cash is required to build the capacity to service that demand. So how much cash will you need?

One of the most important outcomes of the business planning process is to work out how much cash is required to get the business to a specified point.

If the specified point is the first Stability Step, you need to work out what that means in terms of customers and capacity and how much cash would be required to get you there.

You might be wondering what purpose it serves to calculate it when the entry Catch-22 suggests that nobody will help you finance it.

Or you might think that whatever you can afford is all you'll be able to invest – regardless of whether it gets you to the first Stability Step or not.

It all comes down to risk and reward.

If it's a loan, the lender will aim to minimise the risk because the lender's reward is limited to the interest on the debt for the period of the loan. That's why it's normal practice to ask you to put up some form of security, usually your home if you have one.

An investor will usually accept an increased risk, but will expect a greater reward. An investor will also want you to define a timescale for when the investment can be recouped and an estimate of the likely return.

Usually, the faster you want to grow, the bigger the cash requirement and the greater the risk. Hence the difficulty of getting the funding you require, which results in the Entry Catch-22.

So, what should you do to overcome the Entry Catch-22?

The essential strategy is to clearly identify the Stability Step you need to reach and plan the lowest cost and quickest path to get you there.

Working through your business plan helps you identify ways to reduce the level of cash required and the level of risk and then your chances of funding it through whatever means will be increased.

When we investigate how to overcome the Exit Catch-22, we'll look at alternative ways of funding your growth, but at the moment we're dealing with the Entry Catch-22 and we need to concentrate on minimising the amount of cash you might need to get quickly to the first Stability Step.

Here's the core of your strategy to overcome the Entry Catch-22:

1. Customers – use highly effective, but low-cost customer acquisition and customer retention initiatives

2. Capacity – focus on minimising in-house capacity and hence your cash requirement even at the expense of profit.

I cannot emphasise enough the importance of getting this right in the early stages of your business. If you only have a modest amount to invest in your business, put as much as possible into winning customers.

Don't spend your valuable cash on anything that isn't immediately essential.

Outsource absolutely everything you can until you've got your customer pipeline brimming.

The problem is that most enthusiastic new entrepreneurs naturally want to build their tangible infrastructure rather than their more intangible customer base.

But if you really want to succeed – you should put your vanity on a very tight leash for a while.

Success is measured much more by how many customers you have than by how many people you employ, how wonderful your premises appear or the type of car the business owner gets to drive.

I regularly see business owners wanting to move to more prestigious offices or open a showroom or employ people who will not have a direct impact on adding value for the customer. And I often wonder whether this is more for their own vanity or desire to appear successful to their peers than it is a necessity for the business.

It might be necessary for a business to appear successful to its customers to give them the confidence to do business with them. But if the customer will never see the office, it may be an unnecessary burden, especially in the early stages.

Whereas, if your business has vehicles that visit the customer, it may be very worthwhile for these to be relatively new, with the livery of your brand professionally applied and clean and tidy inside and out.

I remember constructing a business plan for a client who was relatively new in business and had great ambition. We had modelled the business, worked out a five-year plan and they had begun implementing it when I received a call.

They had been offered the opportunity to move into better premises and before they accepted they just wanted me to check they could afford the increased costs against the plan.

We had already identified the need for an office move in the plan, but it was another six months away. I ran the numbers on the new rent and then had to explain to the business owners that in my opinion it would put their cashflow under unnecessary pressure. If an impediment hit them it may scupper their dreams.

I suggested that alternative premises will always be available when you need them and to forget about it just now and concentrate on the plan to win customers.

Although reluctant at first, all credit to my client for taking the advice because they not only survived, they moved into new premises on schedule and within two years they expanded again and the business is doing very well.

That business owner still remembers the conversation we had back then and with hindsight recognises how easily they could have made a fatal error and wouldn't be where they are today.

You'll never establish your business and grow rapidly if you're unable to properly fund your marketing and sales because you've absorbed too much of your available cash to fund your capacity.

For a business to be successful, especially in the critical early stages, every activity and expense should be evaluated in terms of its contribution to adding value for the customer and whether the business gets a reasonable return on the expense.

You have to invest in your brand right from the outset. It is an expense that you have to incur, so it's good practise to spend some time thinking it through carefully before you begin pouring cash into promoting it.

The funding required to win customers is often a much larger investment than many business owners expect.

Customers and low-cost customer acquisition

I've lost track of the number of times I've seen business owners wasting their valuable cash on ineffective promotions.

The problem occurs because they don't have a structured marketing plan to deliver the customer numbers required to achieve the objectives of their business plan.

If they have no plan, they're much more likely to be reactive to promotional opportunities and offers as they're presented to them rather than proactively seeking low-cost promotional initiatives.

As a business owner myself, I regularly get unsolicited calls from companies wanting me to take a listing in their business directory, sometimes in paper form and often online. Whilst these may serve a purpose, it has to be in conjunction with a structured promotional plan. Often, they're simply a waste of your valuable cash.

I always recommend my clients to begin with the lowest cost options and work their way up through the cost scale until they achieve the target numbers.

Most forms of general advertising will cost you money regardless of how successful they are at creating demand and hence the opportunity to generate cash.

As a general rule, use them only as a last resort and aim for promotional options that have very little cost or that you only have to pay for if they bring real business.

Definitely don't get suckered into the idea that all promotional activity is good because at the very least it will be building brand awareness.

All your promotional activity has to be effective. Otherwise the cash and your time would have been better spent on alternatives.

And here's another catch for the start-up business. The lowest cost of acquisition for a new customer is likely to be a referral from an existing customer. But the start-up company doesn't have many customers yet, so it gains fewer new customers from this lowest-cost tactic than the more established company.

A start-up has to spend proportionately more on alternative methods when it can least afford it. The more customers you have, as long as you continue to provide great service, the more new business you'll attract through customer referrals.

Recognising this from the outset means you're more likely to place the right level of importance on customer satisfaction.

Only satisfied customers become advocates and provide you with this low-cost way to acquire new customers.

This is why the heart model shows cash flowing out to customer acquisition and retention rather than flowing directly into customers. It's all too easy to burn cash on promotional options that don't deliver the number of customers you require to achieve your growth gradient.

So, what are the low-cost customer acquisition options? The key areas to look at are:

- Viral Marketing – People willingly pass on your Marketing Message with no reward and no reason to track it back to them

- Referral Marketing – Recommendations from customers, suppliers, partners or agents frequently with the means to track it back to them to afford them some benefit even if simply to say thank you

- Internet Marketing – The Internet presents a huge opportunity for small businesses to promote themselves at relatively low cost

- Public Relations (PR) – Editorial or interview coverage via any media.

Each of these is covered in more detail in Part 3, but the main point to remember is that you should identify and implement multiple low-cost options before you consider those options that require greater funding. These may include advertising, telesales, exhibitions, showrooms and sales people.

However, I'm definitely not suggesting that you attempt to create your brand image cheaply. This is one area where you have to spend money to get it done right. Choosing the right name and image is fundamental to your success and there's no point putting a great deal of effort into promoting a brand that's ill conceived.

Here's the test: Ask yourself whether you would be happy with the brand name and image in five years when you've achieved the level of success you desire by then.

If you answer yes – then go ahead and promote it.

If you answer no – are you thinking that you would like to revamp it as soon as you make some money? Well, if you are not happy with it – nobody else will be.

Remember that all the people who might contribute to your success need to believe in you and the brand that you've created.

They are so much more likely to give you their full attention, support and even free help if they believe your brand name has the aura to succeed.

You need to begin with the end in mind and put some real effort and cash into your brand before you do anything else.

Only a well-presented brand image will encourage their belief in you and your brand and enable them to willingly contribute to your success.

All the promotional effort and activity that you undertake prior to changing your brand will be wasted.

Try to create a brand that's future-proof, i.e. it won't age and will still be appropriate if you diversify into alternative markets.

There's lots of advice about how to create a brand, but I'll just share a few tips that I was given:

- It should at least hint at what you do

- It should sound familiar

- It should be easily memorable to aid viral and referral marketing

- It has to be available and not conflict with an existing brand.

We followed this advice when creating the brand for the Business Planning service I established in 2006. The brand we eventually created was Sightpath.

It hints at business planning, because it's about seeing the goal ahead and planning the route to get there. It also sounds familiar in that it's like 'Flight path'.

Unfortunately, it does fall down a little on the viral transmission because although 'sight' and 'site' are easily distinguished when written they sound the same when spoken. If possible try to avoid words that you have to spell out to people because they are less likely to remember it correctly.

If there is a common misspelling of your brand, it may be worth obtaining the web address for the misspelling and making it automatically redirect to your actual web site.

We've briefly covered the first part of the strategy for overcoming the Entry 'Catch-22', low-cost customer acquisition and there's more detail in Part 3.

Now we'll discuss the second part of the strategy, minimising the cost of your capacity.

Capacity and outsourcing

For most businesses, the premier weapon in your armoury for the race to the first Stability Step is likely to be outsourcing.

Of course outsourcing will reduce your profitability, but it can significantly reduce the cash requirement necessary to get you to the first Stability Step.

You might not need to employ as many people so you also may not need as much capital equipment. Any capital equipment that you still require in the early stages can be purchased over a period or leased.

Outsourcing is also a great discipline for making sure your prices are set appropriately right from the outset. Small businesses are notorious for under-pricing, sometimes because the business owners are not factoring the cost of themselves at a proper market rate.

It can be difficult to increase prices once they're established because customers are more likely to feel aggrieved. They might wonder whether they're now being taken for granted if you could do it for a lower price previously.

This may be the trigger to make them investigate alternatives from the competition. And once they start looking – they may like what they see. The art of customer retention is to keep them well-satisfied so they never feel the need to look elsewhere.

There's one other big benefit to outsourcing and that relates to the management of employees. Many business owners have told me that they had never imagined there could be so much bureaucracy and hassle involved in employing people.

They moan about the amount of time it takes to recruit, train and manage people; never mind the dispute resolution.

So, if you're the type of person who recoils from the thought of employing people, outsourcing may solve that problem as well.

I'm not suggesting that outsourcing doesn't present its own set of management issues, but they are different. See the section a little later on outsourcing issues.

Now let's reflect on how outsourcing can work. First we'll consider a product-based business that needs to hold and dispatch stock.

Outsourcing for a product-based business

One of my clients was a start-up business that had outsourced the manufacture and packaging of their entire product range, but was then agonising over the size of the warehouse space they would need. This depended on the level of success they might achieve when marketing the brand and the products. However, at this stage they didn't know how successful they would be and what level of stock they would need to hold and therefore, what size warehouse to rent.

I suggested that they could go even further with their outsourcing to include the whole distribution and logistics side of the business as well. This can then scale easily to match your marketing success.

Instead of funding your own warehouse and logistics, you can outsource to an external 'fulfilment' company. These companies run warehousing on behalf of many companies.

Effectively, you're sharing the costs with other companies so that when one warehouse guy gets sick there are still others to get the stock off the shelves and ship it to the customers.

Most fulfilment companies will also take your customer orders and invoice your customers directly on your behalf without the customer ever knowing it wasn't your company.

You will still have to buy the stock and get it delivered to the fulfilment company and you will still have to fund the marketing of your brand and its products.

Initially, it may be wise to buy in small batches at the expense of profit to reduce your cash requirement and to ensure you have enough cash to fund your marketing and drive your sales pipeline.

Although outsourcing is usually at the expense of profit, it is much better for your cashflow and that is more critical.

Referring back to the 'S' curve of business growth, at the early stages cash is more important than profit whereas when the growth slows off at the top of the curve, you can concentrate on maximising profit. Companies would then explore whether outsourcing remains appropriate.

Outsourcing for a service-based business

Now we'll consider a service-based business that requires three types of resources to service its customers.

Suppose that the number of hours required of each resource to service a typical customer is as shown in the table below.

Resource Type	Number of hours
Type A	6
Type B	3
Type C	2

You can't service a customer without having all three resource types available, but you would need 2 'A's for every 'B' and 3 'A's for every 'C'.

The first Stability Step would occur when you have no under-utilisation and at least two of every resource type to give some cover for absence?

In our example, this would not occur until you had 2 'C's, 3 'B's and 6 'A's giving a total resource requirement of 11. Not only is this a high number of staff to fund, train, support and accommodate from day one, but you would also have to fund extensive marketing to deliver enough sales to keep them all fully utilised.

However, if you could outsource the type 'C' resource, you would only need 2 'B's and 4 'A's to have cover for each type of resource, which would reduce your initial requirement to 6.

And what if you could outsource both 'B's and 'C's – would you be able to get away with just two 'A's and still be at a Stability Step? It will probably depend on the type of business.

I have a client who runs several Physiotherapy and Sports Massage clinics. She leases the premises and has them kitted out with treatment rooms. She is an expert in the field and has developed the brand and promotes it.

This business model requires a 'big bang' approach, but the business only directly employs the Practice Administrator and receptionists at each location. The treatment is provided by clinicians who are not employed by the company, they work for themselves.

The fee the clients pay is shared between the practice and the clinicians, but each clinician is only paid for the treatment they provide.

The business model keeps the costs of the capacity under control because the business doesn't have to pay for under-utilised clinicians. It means they can make a profit with only half their treatment rooms being utilised. This will help the business survive impediments and even an economic downturn.

Outsourcing issues

As well as a reduction in profitability, there are some other primary concerns that business owners have with regard to outsourcing:

1. Profit margin

2. Controlling service levels

3. Losing the customer directly to the outsource provider.

Let's deal with these one at a time.

Profit margin

It's actually very good discipline to see whether your business can operate with as much outsourced as possible. If you get your proposition right such that it is viable using outsourcing, your business will be all the stronger when you are in a position to bring it in-house.

For example, as mentioned in the section regarding the first measure of success, I see many business owners working in their business without drawing a proper wage for themselves.

Imagine if you attempted to outsource part of the work that you undertake as the business owner and found a company keen for your business and you asked them if they would be prepared to do it at half the market rate. I think we can anticipate the reply.

In the course of my work I'm often having to show business owners that they need to increase their prices. Outsourcing is a good way to check the value you're providing and help price your product or service correctly.

Even if you decide not to outsource, getting quotations from possible suppliers of the various services can help you check the price you should be charging and whether your customers would perceive that price as appropriate for the value added.

If you really don't think your margins can stand outsourcing then you should be concerned whether your business would be in a position to withstand an economic downturn or any of the impediments that tend to take out a business in the early stages.

If you think your business is in this position I would recommend that you refine your business proposition to specialise in a niche market. The benefit is that you will be able to hone your products and services and your infrastructure towards satisfying your specific customer base and improve the value you add.

Focusing on a niche also helps you target your promotional activity more accurately and improve customer acquisition and retention. Efficiency will improve and your profitability will increase.

Consider the example of the personal computer market. As the manufacture of PCs has continued to spread globally and supply easily outstrips demand, profit margins continue to shrink.

IBM has completely pulled out of the PC market to concentrate on big machines and business services.

Apple Macintosh targeted a specific niche and has been able to maintain its position and its margins. They designed their hardware and software applications to appeal specifically to the creative and design sectors. This has enabled Apple to maintain a premium price and their position of market leader within their niche.

There really is little point in putting a lot of effort and money into a venture with thin profit margins. You'll always be at the mercy of increased global competition or simply a run of minor impediments conspiring against you.

If you can achieve the first Stability Step by focusing on a niche, you can always expand your horizons from a position of strength.

Controlling service levels

It is often a misconception that you would be able to offer a better service, especially if your business is very small.

This is because a small business finds it more difficult to cover for absences. A small company can often struggle to provide acceptable service levels even when others are willing to work excessive hours to compensate.

A small company will also struggle during times when demand peaks, so if your business is seasonal or demand fluctuates significantly, it can be more difficult to manage with only a small team.

You should choose an outsource provider that you believe will endeavour to provide the best service they can to retain your business. You can also put measures in place to monitor service levels and if they don't match up you can take your business elsewhere.

Try to select a service provider where your business is reasonably significant to them and you'll be more able to dictate improvements.

Losing control of the customer

The other concern many small businesses have with outsourcing is they fear they may lose control of the customer. They wonder what will prevent the customer cutting them out of the loop and going directly to the outsource company.

This is why you have to break your proposition down in terms of value.

At every point along the chain where cost is added – commensurate value must be added for the customer.

For example, in terms of a product: a company takes raw materials and adds design and manufacturing skills to create an end product that is worth more to the customer than the constituent parts.

If you provide a service you have to be clear about the expertise your business adds to create value for the customer to justify your position in the chain and the cost added.

There is no fixed amount of money in circulation in our economy and there is no fixed amount of value being contributed by businesses. So, if you take up a position in the value chain, you are not necessarily depriving someone else of their slice.

If your business is really adding value then your position is justified, however, if you're not adding value there's nothing to prevent the customer from cutting you out of the loop.

OK, so let's assume you are adding value to your customers – do you need to be concerned about customers cutting you out of the loop and going directly to the outsourced company?

The key issue is whether you're offering value for your management of the outsourced part of the total service being provided by your business.

If you're going to outsource part of your service, you must be very clear about how you would like your brand to be perceived by the customer and how this might be affected by outsourcing.

You also need to decide whether the customer should be fully aware of the fact that you're outsourcing or whether it is merely an internal capacity issue that should be of little concern to the customer as long as the work gets completed correctly.

Let's look at a couple of examples:

Example 1: Building contractor

A client of mine is a builder, but he doesn't actually do the building work himself. He's very good at winning the business and managing the customer and he employs teams of builders who are good at doing the work, but are less able to engage in dialogue with the customers.

The customer knows that my client is taking 10%, but appreciates the value of the role that he performs.

I remember him telling me of the occasion when one of his customers fell out with the building team assigned and it was irreconcilable. If this were to happen in a normal situation the customer would really struggle to find a new builder willing to take on another builder's stalled project. And if one did agree, the customer would almost certainly have to pay more than the original price.

However, because of my client's contract management role, he was able to switch teams without the customer being inconvenienced beyond a few weeks delay. The new team was obliged to take on a project that was already underway because the pipeline of work my client was consistently providing to them was very significant to their business.

He offers a point of mediation and he is able to explain to the customer more easily on the occasions when the building team is actually doing the right thing and the customer has not grasped the situation properly.

My client's 10% fee provides value in the same way that an insurance policy does – even if you never claim. He is someone who understands the situation from the customer's perspective and knows the importance of customer satisfaction and how essential it is if you want them to recommend you to others.

Example 2: Domestic cleaning company

Another of my clients provides domestic cleaning services and my wife and I actually use their weekly cleaning service for our own home. Their business doesn't directly employ the cleaners, they outsource to hundreds of individuals. And here's the interesting point – we pay the cleaner directly each week and we pay the company by monthly standing order for their management fee.

Sometimes we've had a specific cleaner reliably serving us for more than a year and the company appears to have provided no value for their fee.

So, why do we keep paying their management fee?

It's because we don't want any hassle.

It is the company that provides insurance in case the cleaner breaks something, or trips and is injured in our home, or leaves the house insecure and we're burgled.

It is the company that recruits and checks a replacement when required so that we have no hassle.

But perhaps the best reason was demonstrated when my wife's parents were coming for the weekend. My mother-in-law always keeps an immaculate house, whereas our two children seem much keener to adopt the opposite approach.

My wife and I both work and we were relying on our cleaner's regular visit on the Thursday to prepare the house for their arrival on Friday afternoon.

When we returned home on Thursday we found the house hadn't been cleaned and there was an apology on the answer phone from our cleaner saying she was sick and would not be coming that day.

I immediately called the cleaning company and explained our predicament and they arranged for a different cleaner to come the following morning. They quickly resolved our problem and justified their management fee.

What if outsourcing isn't an option?

There is nearly always some element of the business that can be outsourced.

There may be some businesses where outsourcing isn't immediately an option because the required skill doesn't exist in the market.

However, it may be possible to train people to do the work, but still not employ them. They may be part of a larger company or they may be individuals.

The important point is that you pay them only for the work they actually undertake and minimise any under-utilisation.

You may be able to operate a quasi franchise approach. Recruit agents that do the work for you for a commission or pay you a commission for using your system, methodology or branding.

If you really need to employ people, you could offer a salary below the market rate in return for a bonus element that would allow them to earn above the market rate on results.

If you have no choice but to employ your capacity on your pay roll at full market rate, the 'big bang' strategy is still the best option for success, but you'll have to access enough investment to fund both your capacity and your customer acquisition plan.

There are some advantages when employing several people together as against the more cautious option of first one and then later another.

For example, it will enable you to:

- Leverage your recruitment costs
- Leverage your training effort
- Create a self-help environment
- Compare and stimulate their performance
- Go for a 'bigger bang' promotional push without fear of not being able to cope.

There will be occasions when you find that you've made an inappropriate recruitment choice, so ideally you should protect yourself by having a probation period in your contract of employment.

There are free templates for contracts of employment available on the Internet, although if your business is particularly unusual you may need to seek advice from a specialist employment advisor.

It's not just small start-ups that have to enter at a Stability Step using the 'big bang' approach and might reduce their cash requirements through the outsource option.

Consider the example of a new mobile phone service provider. To provide a service that can compete with existing providers a new entrant would need to somehow offer nationwide signal capacity right from the outset.

This would require a huge investment to create the network of transceivers before you could achieve a single sale. A sensible approach may be to lease capacity from existing providers.

What about starting a new airline? A while back I knew of a group of dentists who collectively put some of their earnings into buying a passenger jet and then leased it to a major airline. Although it cost many millions to buy, it represented a good return-on-investment because the airline would lease it for several years; after all, they had to have it painted with their branding.

It represented a good option for the airline because there was no requirement to find the upfront cash when they needed the reserves to cover their operating costs.

Strategy for overcoming the Entry Catch-22

To beat the Entry Catch-22 you should minimise your cash requirement even at the expense of profit. The more you can do this, the lower the amount of cash you need to get you quickly to a Stability Step.

This means the amount you may need to fund from an external source will be reduced.

Not only that, but showing how the funding will get you to a Stability Step will encourage a lender or investor to believe that the risk will be lower and this will improve your chances of getting it.

Wherever possible add your capacity infrastructure only after you've got your customer pipeline brimming. Until then, outsource everything you possibly can.

Use your valuable cash primarily on building your brand and investing in customer acquisition.

There are some businesses where you have to add the capacity from the outset. For such businesses you should begin the marketing process as early as possible before taking on capacity and fully launching. This will minimise your cash requirement.

As we move onto the other Catch-22s, you will see how the strategy we've discussed will help overcome those as well. As I mentioned earlier, you will soon appreciate the extent to which they are all inter-dependent.

Entry Phase Summary

1. Work out a stability threshold for your business, i.e. the point where you are able to efficiently utilise your capacity without inconveniencing your customers when impediments occur. Then focus all your efforts exclusively on getting there.

2. The 'big bang' approach to reaching the first Stability Step offers the quickest way to lift your business out of the survival zone and increase your chances of success.

3. Presenting an aura of success and a go-for-it attitude will attract people to support and contribute to your success, sometimes for minimal or no charge.

4. Properly plan and fund your customer acquisition activities and don't spend valuable cash on unsolicited advertising opportunities.

5. On your way to the first Stability Step outsource as much of your capacity as possible, even at the expense of profit.

The Growth Phase

The Growth Dilemma is the decision when to go for profit and the Growth Catch-22 is about finding the right balance as you grow, defined as follows:

Your level of funding dictates your growth gradient and hence your future earnings – yet it is your future earnings that will define the level of funding worth investing.

We discussed earlier how growth usually takes the form of an 'S' curve and that for most businesses growth is a succession of 'S' curves.

Each growth phase will have its own 'hockey stick' profile for cumulative cash, which may require the investment of additional funds; and the steeper the growth gradient – the deeper the cash requirement.

In between each growth phase there are points of stability. What might these points of stability be for your business?

Referring to the heart model, your Stability Steps might be primarily driven by Customers with Capacity scaled to match or driven by Capacity limitations with Customers scaled to match.

For example, if the catchment area of your business is restricted to a certain size, the market for your services is also restricted and when the competition is taken into account there is likely to be a limit to the market share that it is realistic to target. The Capacity should be scaled to match the market share target.

Alternatively, if there is a limit to Capacity e.g. for a certain size of building and the numbers of resources that can be accommodated, the Customers should then be scaled to match.

Visualise the heart model on its fulcrum and when you make a business decision ask yourself whether it could put the heart out of balance in favour of customers or capacity? Usually, it will, but for how long?

During growth phases, the heart of business success tends to heel over as you add chunks of capacity. The more it heels over the more cash it will be haemorrhaging and the more likely it will be fatal for the business.

If you are fortunate enough to be in a market that has no physical constraints or market share constraints, the Stability Steps may be much more difficult to calculate.

In this case you should identify a point where customers and capacity are efficiently matched and you have the cash to fund the acquisition of the customer numbers required and fund the infrastructure to support the capacity to match.

You might be able to identify the various Stability Steps that make sense for your business right from the start. This is likely to be the case for capacity-driven businesses.

The more established the business, the greater its ability to attract additional investment. So the various growth phases are not necessarily of similar gradients; they may get progressively steeper as shown in the figure below:

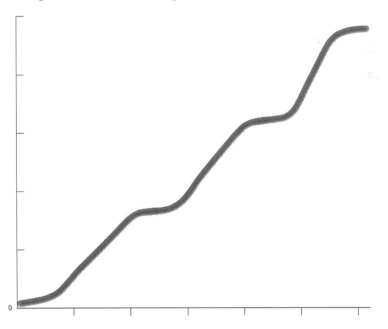

Different Growth Gradients for different phases

Your business plan can now indicate how you will achieve your long-term goals in broad outline and show how you plan to reach the next Stability Step in detail.

You can then revise your business plan every time you achieve the next Stability Step.

Deciding when to profit

If you're trying to reach the first Stability Step this is not the right time to go for profit. Try to minimise the cost of your infrastructure and direct funds to building your brand and your customer acquisition.

Once you've reached the first Stability Step, you have the option to bring more of your outsourced infrastructure in-house to improve your profitability.

In the start-up phase and in any of the subsequent growth phases, it is cash that is most critical even at the expense of profit.

Focus on cash when you're ascending and as you reach any of the Stability Steps you can concentrate on maximising profit.

But if you don't plan to remain on a particular Stability Step for very long, it may be wise to keep your focus on cash ready for the next ascent.

Plan your overall growth strategy in the same way that you would plan an assent on a mountain. Think of base camp as the first Stability Step. Work out what you plan to achieve for each phase of the assent to the next Stability Step all the way to the summit of your ambition.

Then you can focus on getting as far as the next Stability Step one at time.

This strategy will maximise your chances of success because even if you encounter an impediment or bad economic weather you will know how to reach the nearest Stability Step where you can shelter and recuperate.

When you're on or near a Stability Step, you can begin to switch your focus to profitability.

The Growth Dilemma decision to maximise profit becomes clearer if you can identify the various Stability Steps for your business.

I remember working with a client who had a varied resource structure requiring several different complementary skills. To satisfy the needs of their customers they required quite varied amounts of the different skills.

Like most businesses they were keen to grow and had assumed it would be a fairly linear progression. They had broadly identified their ambition for the business and without realising it they were not far away from achieving the first Stability Step.

When I modelled the business, I was able to show them the significance of reaching the first Stability Step. The efficiency they would achieve by reaching the Stability Step would have a big impact on their profitability and for the first time they would at last be able to pay themselves appropriately for their efforts.

This meant that if they achieved the first Stability Step, they would also achieve the first measure of success that we derived in Part 1. The two owners would be able to pay themselves at a rate equal or greater than they would be able to achieve working for another company.

It is so often the case that these two points coincide because up until the first Stability Step the business isn't sufficiently profitable for the owners to draw appropriate earnings.

This is a valuable example because of the complexity of their resource types. It was this complexity that meant they had employed a significant number of people in comparison to their customer base and sales potential.

Cash had to be available to pay all these salaries before it could pay the owners. In contrast to many larger companies the bosses of many small businesses are unable to pay themselves more than their employees.

But the main reason I wanted to introduce this example is because when we modelled the business we found that the next Stability Step was a considerable. The business didn't operate in a vast market, so reaching it would require a significant increase in their market share.

This gave the owners some critical information to enable them to make the most appropriate business decisions. They now realised the danger if they continued to add capacity that took them beyond the next Stability Step. They would return to under-utilisation, which would reduce their efficiency and hence reduce profitability.

They had two clear options to consider:

1. Go for growth and push hard to reach the next Stability Step and accept the challenge of funding a big increase in customer acquisition initiatives

2. Remain at the first Stability Step and go for maximising profit and run a good comfortable business that can pay them well enough to fund a pension plan.

These decisions only became clear because we were able to calculate the various Stability Steps for the business. You can see how it enables you to make the right choice based on knowledge rather than blindly going forward.

If they had not realised the significance of the next Stability Step and simply tried to grow incrementally, they could find themselves with poor profitability for some time. Not only is this demoralising for the owners as it limits their personal income, but it also leaves the business more vulnerable.

Understanding this also helps us to consider alternative options. In this case the most obvious one is to seek a merger. And the conversation immediately began to speculate as to the likely candidates.

A strategy to merge wouldn't ordinarily have arrived on the agenda.

The heart model shows the importance of keeping Customers, Capacity and Cash in balance as you grow. This helps us to realise that growth is not necessarily linear and to seek Stability Steps where we can strive to increase profits.

So, now you can make decisions about when to profit and answer the Growth Dilemma.

Overcoming the Growth Catch-22

The Growth Catch-22 is defined as follows:

Your level of funding dictates your growth gradient and hence your future earnings – yet it is your future earnings that will define the level of funding worth investing.

Your level of funding dictates your growth gradient and future earnings

Your future earnings define the level of funding worth investing

The Growth Catch-22 can lead to the 'Saw-tooth' profile where you're expending all the effort and receiving none of the reward.

You need to find an appropriate balance between ambition and funding for each growth phase that will get you to the next Stability Step.

This requires you to define your Ambition Aim with a Time Target to define your desired Growth Gradient and then calculate your cash requirement.

If you can't fund or don't feel comfortable funding the cash requirement for the declared Growth Gradient you can either reduce your Ambition Aim or extend your Time Target.

You may wonder why I'm using 'Ambition' and 'Aim' together when either word might suffice. I find the word 'ambition' on its own to be an expression of a desire and although the word 'aim' implies a clear target, it can apply to anything. Using them together seems to overcome this problem and for me, creates a better emphasis.

When I'm speaking to business groups I sometimes use the following method to illustrate the importance of setting a clear ambition and then aiming at it:

First I ask for a volunteer – there's always someone willing to put themselves forward, even when they don't know what's coming next.

I ask the volunteer to stand up and point to someone else in the audience.

Then I take a piece of paper, screw it up and throw it in the general direction of the nominated person. It's unusual for the guest speaker to throw paper balls at the audience, so I have their full attention when I explain:

"OK, so I might not have got it exactly where you pointed, but I got a lot closer than if I'd merely thrown it aimlessly in the air. And it's the same with your business – you're more likely to hit what you aim at."

Once you know what you're aiming at, you can develop strategies to hit it.

When you know what your strategies are, you can estimate the amount of cash you'll need to invest in order to hit your Ambition Aim.

As mentioned earlier, you can have different Growth Gradients on the way to each of the various Stability Steps. So the term Ambition Aim could be used as a target to achieve a specific Stability Step on the way to your overall ambition.

It can relate to the immediate ambition that you're currently planning to achieve within a specific timescale.

You can think of your overall ambition, which may be some way off, as a force 'pulling' and guiding you up the mountain towards the summit and think of each Ambition Aim as the effort you have to apply now to 'push' you upwards.

Unfortunately, it can take so long to calculate the cash requirement for each Ambition Aim that the tendency is to not go back and rework the figures when you need to make adjustments; for example because you find the cash requirement is more than you expected.

If you don't rework the figures you'll find it difficult to balance your ambition and your funding, which can lead to the 'Saw-tooth' effect and flat lining.

It's so normal for the cash requirement to be more than expected that the 'Saw-tooth' effect seems to be the usual outcome. If you want to be one of the few to break free and properly grow, you have to calculate the cash requirement and if you can't fund it, make adjustments and re-calculate until you find a balance between ambition and funding.

There is a solution to the problem of calculating the cash requirement and I've been using it to great effect with my clients. I use the following two stage process:

1. Create a business model where the scale of ambition can be adjusted easily

2. Run your model until you find a balance between ambition and funding.

With this method, we can first explore ways to reduce the cash requirement without reducing the scale of ambition. For example, by outsourcing more of what you do or by leasing the equipment that enables you to do what you do. Or by using one of the Alternative Finance Options covered later under the section on overcoming the Exit catch-22.

If you can't reduce the cash requirement and therefore the funding needed to achieve your desired Growth Gradient you can look at scaling back your Ambition Aim or extending your Time Target.

So how do we create a business model where the scale of ambition can be adjusted easily? We refer to the heart of business success to help us.

The heart model displays three critical 'C's, Customers, Capacity and Cash and there are four links between these as shown by the numbers overlaid on the heart in the figure below:

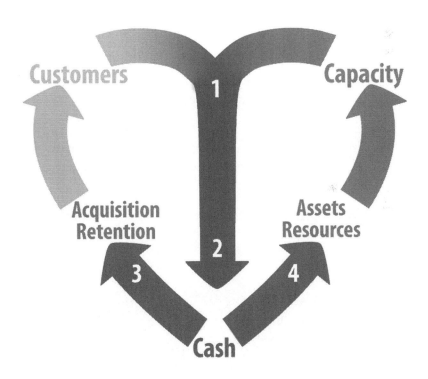

The heart model showing numbered links between the three critical 'C's: Customers, Capacity and Cash

You can use these four links to create a business model and calculate your cash requirement for a specific Ambition Aim, Time Target and Growth Gradient:

1. Link Customers to Capacity – What infrastructure is required to service all your different types of customers and how does this change as customer numbers grow.

2. Link Customers to Cash 'in' – Cash is received according to the behaviour of different customer types, i.e. what they buy and how frequently they tend to buy.

3. Link Customer Acquisition to Cash 'out' – The amount of cash needed to acquire new customers depends on the desired Growth Gradient and the rate of Customer Retention, i.e. how long they continue to buy.

4. Link Capacity to Cash 'out' – The amount of cash required for fixed overheads to support your capacity and for the costs of capacity scaled to service your growing customer numbers.

Begin by creating these links without considering the scale of the business. This means you are modelling the relationships between Customers, Capacity and Cash.

Once you've created the business model, you can experiment with scale, i.e. how much cash would you have to invest to achieve the Growth Gradient required for your desired Ambition Aim and Time Target?

You may need to consider whether you need to augment your range of products or services or whether you need to move into alternative markets.

We'll now take a look at each of these links in more detail.

Link 1: Customers to Capacity

There's a good reason why the first link describes the relationship between customers and capacity – and that's because this is the link that defines what the business actually does. It details the means by which a business is able to provide solutions to satisfy the needs of its customers.

Of course, just because a customer has a need doesn't mean you have to satisfy it.

There seems to be a natural tendency for small companies to try to deliver whatever customers want.

We seem to have a natural aversion to saying 'no' – yet 'no' may be exactly what needs to be said in order to maintain customer satisfaction levels. When you agree to something outside your normal range of capability you run the risk that you will under-perform.

It's important to do what you do well before you extend the scope of what you do.

You should carefully consider exactly what the scope of your capability will be and then regularly review it. If you see the opportunity to extend it you should take time to properly consider the size of the potential market and whether it's worth investing in the extended capability.

Success is more likely if you have the necessary expertise, equipment and capacity to provide a particular solution and your company remains enthusiastic about wanting to deliver it and you do so consistently well.

Link 1 requires you to define the capability your business currently offers or plans to offer within the period under consideration.

For a service-based business this link defines the amount of time typically required to satisfy the different services offered to your different types of customers by your different types of resources. This enables you to work out how many of each type of resource you will require as your customer numbers increase.

For a product-based business this link defines the different batch sizes available and unit costs. This enables you to work out the impact on cash flow as you buy stock to service your growing customer numbers.

This is essential information to calculate the various Stability Steps for your business as it grows.

Link 2: Customers to Cash

This is the link between different customer types and receipt of cash. This link enables you to calculate the typical order value. If customers tend to make regular repeat purchases, you will also need to estimate the repeat purchase frequency.

Now you can calculate how many customers you need at each point along your Growth Gradient towards your Ambition Aim.

This is also the link where you investigate your pricing policy. As mentioned earlier, small businesses tend to price very keenly and are sometimes too quick to discount in order to win business.

The type of business model that is derived by considering the heart of business success helps you to relate the number of customers required to achieve your sales targets, but this can change dramatically if you regularly offer discounts.

Let me illustrate this with an example. Suppose the gross margin on a product is 50% and you propose to offer a discount of just 10%. You will have to sell 25% more product to provide you with the same cash as you would if you gave no discount. If you gave away 15% discount you would have to sell an incredible 43% more just to stand still in terms of cash received.

Discounting is less critical for service-based businesses because their gross margins tend to be much higher.

Many of my clients are very nervous about the effect on sales of increasing their prices. So, let's look at the same example where a product has a 50% gross margin.

If you were to put your prices up by 10%, you can sell 17% fewer and still receive the same cash as you would if you had not raised the price. If you put your prices up by 15% you can sell 23% fewer and still receive the same cash.

But there may be implications that go beyond the effect on link 2 of our model.

If you sell fewer items, you may be able to release some capacity either in the form of stock or people. This would improve your net profitability and could significantly reduce your cash requirement.

Alternatively, the extra capacity could be used to serve more customers without an increase in infrastructure enabling you to grow faster with the same cash requirement.

Again, this shows how everything in business is inter-related. Creating a business model with the four links shown on the heart of business success enables you to work through these connections and plan how to achieve greater ambition in a shorter time yet remain in balance.

Link 3: Customer Acquisition to Cash 'out'

This link forms the basis of your Marketing Plan and enables you to estimate the size of the promotional budget required to attain the numbers of customers required to achieve your ambition.

Begin with the lowest cost acquisition options first. It always costs more to kick start a new growth phase and as you grow you will hopefully benefit more from customer referrals. As long as you maintain good levels of customer satisfaction as you grow.

Not all businesses have customers that make regular repeat purchases.

If repeat purchases are infrequent your business model can assume that all sales will be expected to be derived from new customer acquisition. For this type of business there can never be any let up in customer acquisition initiatives because there is a direct link to sales.

For those companies that derive a large proportion of their sales from repeat purchases the rate of customer retention is an important consideration.

The better your customer retention the lower your customer acquisition rate needs to be to achieve your growth gradient.

Alternatively, with a better customer retention rate you can grow faster for the same customer acquisition rate.

If you direct some attention and often some cash into customer satisfaction to improve retention the level of both your attention and cash can frequently be recouped several times over. This is because you can show high levels of customer satisfaction, which will improve your rate of new customer acquisition.

This is why the heart of business success shows both Acquisition and Retention as part of link 3.

Customer Retention

When you consider how difficult and expensive it can be to acquire a new customer, it seems incredible that companies don't make every effort to keep their existing customers satisfied and retain them for as long as possible.

You would expect it to be good practice to focus on retention even more diligently than acquisition.

So why don't small companies have great customer retention policies?

It seems to be a problem of order – you have to attain customers before you can retain them.

When a company starts it doesn't have any customers and has to focus on the means to acquire them. At this point, it seems irrelevant to discuss retention policies when you don't have any customers to retain.

Once a company is trading and getting busier, there never seems to be the time to establish a structured approach to customer satisfaction and retention.

For those businesses where repeat buying by existing customers is a large part of revenue generation it is important to include the rate of customer retention in your model.

If you assume all customers remain with you forever you will vastly under-estimate the number of new customers you need to acquire to achieve your desired growth gradient. You may not budget enough cash to fund your customer acquisition and the whole business may be put at risk.

Perhaps this is another reason why many small businesses fail; because they don't correctly estimate the number of new customers they need to acquire and hence the amount of cash required for link 3 of the heart model.

Let's take a moment to consider the reasons customers may leave, not all of these will be relevant depending on whether you generally sell to other businesses or directly to the public:

- A customer moves location and decides to source an alternative supplier locally

- A customer is dissatisfied with your product or service and decides to switch suppliers

- A customer simply no longer requires the product or service, e.g. the babies have all grown up

- A customer mirrors the lifecycle of your product and the replacements in your range are not chosen

- A business customer adjusts its market position and no longer requires your product or service

- A business customer is in decline and demand for your product or service is shrinking.

As you can see from this short list many of the reasons a customer may leave are outside of your control, so it doesn't matter how good your customer service levels are you still can't escape the need to attract new customers.

I always ask my new clients about their customer retention rate and sometimes without hesitation they'll tell me that it's one hundred per cent. When this happens, I usually pause and look sceptical. They usually feel slightly embarrassed when they realise how unlikely it sounds and make a correction. *"Well maybe it's more like ninety percent, but it's very high".*

Perhaps the reason many people are over-optimistic about customer retention is because we don't like to focus on our failings. But this is one area where some focus can make a big difference.

Customers tend to bleat about grievances to others more readily than they rave about good service. So, if customers are defecting because of dissatisfaction it not only means the business loses valuable customers, it quite often damages its reputation as well.

This is likely to have an impact on customer acquisition, which will increase the level of investment required for link 3.

If your business has repeat purchasing from customers, devise strategies to improve customer retention and integrate them within your processes and systems. There is more on customer retention in Part 3

Link 4: Capacity to Cash 'out'

There are two types of ongoing costs that absorb your cash:

1. Fixed overheads

2. Scaled overheads.

Fixed overheads refer to the costs incurred whether you have one customer or many customers. Examples of Fixed Overheads include the costs of certain employees such as the Managing Director and Receptionist as well as infrastructure costs such as the rent and rates for premises.

As a business grows, its fixed overheads will be amortised over more and more customers and have less of an impact. Fixed overheads are still likely to increase as a business grows, for example when it moves into larger premises.

Scaled overheads refer to those that increase in line with growing customer numbers, for example the costs of employees that directly service customers. These are still referred to as overheads to differentiate them from Direct Costs, which are costs that can be attributed directly to sales, for example the costs of the products being traded.

Once you know how many customers you need at each point along your growth gradient you can use the information in Link 1 to estimate when you will need to fund employing more of each resource type required to service them.

Or for a Product-based business you can estimate when you will need to fund additional stock.

There will also be some Capital Expenditure to fund assets, for example vehicles, equipment, computers, software systems and web site.

Some businesses can dramatically increase the efficiency of servicing customers by the introduction of systems. It may be that a business has to reach a certain size before it becomes appropriate to spend the cash on buying or developing appropriate systems.

Funding new systems can be a clear reason for obtaining finance because the increased efficiency would translate into extra profits to pay back the loan. You would be able to calculate how long it would take to break-even on the investment and then to reap additional profits from there on.

Running your business model

Once you've created all these links, you can enter the customer numbers needed to achieve a particular Ambition Aim within a Time Target, which defines your Growth Gradient.

The model will show your flow of cash in and out of the business as it grows and give you an estimate of your most negative cumulative cash requirement.

This is the extent of funding that will be required to service the Growth Gradient.

You can run the model several times experimenting with different numbers of customers for different Ambition Aims and Time Targets each time check the cumulative cash requirement.

This process enables you to keep Customers and Capacity in balance as you grow and avoid the heart tipping over on its Cash pivot point – in either the direction of Capacity or the direction of Customers.

Because you've calculated the extent of your cash requirement for your Growth Gradient it won't come as a surprise and you can plan for it.

Remember that a cashflow problem is usually an unforeseen cash requirement.

Once you've worked out a good balance for *you* and checked whether your business or business idea at least has the potential to achieve your ambition, you then have the following reality check to perform.

Are there sufficient numbers of customers in your target market for you to achieve your Ambition Aim taking into account the level of competition already present?

Market Analysis

A few simple calculations should always be made before you embark on a new venture or a new growth phase to check that the opportunity is sufficiently scalable to deliver against your expectations.

For example, suppose you want to set up a hair salon. Most people will use a hair salon near to where they live or work, so you can define an appropriate geographic region for your market.

Estimate the likely client base for your target demographic group and estimate the total numbers and potential market revenues. Check the number of salons already operating in your defined region and within your target market.

Your new salon will have to compete against the existing salons for a share of the market. If the total number of salons would be around twenty and all things are equal you can reasonably expect to grow to around 5% of the market.

You might be able to slightly exceed the average market share by employing some highly talented stylists or some great customer service ideas. But remember, these may only be short lived because no business operates in isolation and if your competitors see you being successful they will inevitably copy your initiatives.

If the turnover target necessary to reach your ambition would require you to achieve 25% of the market, you would have to own five of the salons in the region. How feasible is that within your timescale? If not, you can choose to reduce the level of your ambition or you can find an alternative business proposition.

If your ambition remains out of balance with reality there is simply no chance of success.

This is the process I have employed on many occasions to help small businesses plan for success.

A client of mine first made contact after he'd been refused a loan by several of the major banks and was extremely frustrated by their lack of support.

As is so often the case, none of the banks had explained why his application had been rejected.

He'd used his own cash to develop a new product and get the first batch manufactured. He'd also successfully promoted the product and persuaded the market of the need. He had actually managed to completely sell the first batch and so he felt that he'd proved the viability of the product and his business.

He'd now exhausted his cash reserves and wanted the loan to buy more stock and increase his marketing efforts.

Together we created a model of the business using the heart of business success concept as we've discussed and began looking at how we would scale his ambition and the level of funding he would need.

Very soon it became apparent that the market was not sufficiently large to be able to achieve his ambitions for the business.

I asked him whether he could develop some additional products.

He explained that he had many product development ideas, but he had assumed that it would be better to get the business established first by trading the product he'd already developed.

As this did not appear to be viable he would need to launch a range of products from the outset, so that the business infrastructure and marketing expenses would be amortised across a range of products.

I suspect the banks had reached a similar conclusion, probably more through experienced intuition than any in depth analysis.

This makes it more difficult for them to explain and justify their decision, which contributes to the frustration experienced by loan applicants.

We spent some time adding the new product ideas to the business model and found that the business viability was transformed.

We amended the business plan and he went back to the same banks with the revised business plan and they all agreed to sanction the loan.

Using the four links shown on the heart model to calculate the cash requirement for a growth gradient is the process for overcoming the Growth Catch-22 and keeping your ambition and funding in balance as you grow.

Business owners tend to underestimate the extent of time and funding that is required to achieve the customer numbers required to achieve their ambition.

Your business plan should incorporate a marketing plan to show how you intend to attain the customer numbers required to achieve your ambition. This is covered in more detail in Part 3.

Growth Phase Summary

1. Plan your overall growth strategy in the same way that you would plan an assent on a mountain. Think of base camp as the first Stability Step. Work out what you plan to achieve for each phase of the assent to the next Stability Step all the way to the summit of your ambition.

2. During growth phases, the heart of business success tends to heel over as you add chunks of capacity. The more it heels over the more cash it will be haemorrhaging and the more likely it will be fatal for the business.

3. Focus on cash when you're in the vulnerable ascent and on profit as you arrive at a Stability Step.

4. Find an appropriate balance between ambition and funding for each growth phase that will get you to the next Stability Step. Define your Ambition Aim, Time Target and Growth Gradient with a cash requirement you know you can fund.

5. Use the 4 links between the 3 Critical 'C's on the heart of business success to create a business model to calculate the cash requirement for a particular Ambition Aim and Time Target.

6. Undertake a Market Analysis to check that there are sufficient numbers of customers in your target market for you to achieve your Ambition Aim taking into account the level of competition already present.

7. Most small businesses under-estimate the effort required to attract new customers. Include a comprehensive marketing plan within your business plan. Employ low cost promotional options first.

8. If your business has repeat purchasing from customers, devise strategies to improve customer retention.

The Exit Phase

The Exit Dilemma is deciding when you should exit your business and the Exit Catch-22 is about financing your ambition and the impact of that finance on the value you obtain when you exit.

What do you need your business to be worth and in what timescale?

If you focus on building business value from the outset, you're more likely to be one of the elite few to succeed.

Ideally, you will plan ahead for your exit, the point at which you would like to sell your business. If you plan ahead you're more likely to achieve the best business valuation within your time frame.

As with anything, a business is only worth what someone is prepared to pay for it. So, it is important to direct your business strategy and business plan at maximising the value of your business to the people most likely to buy it.

In order to know how to maximise the valuation of your business you need to understand how businesses tend to be valued. So let's take a look at the various common techniques.

There are several ways to value a business:

- Entry cost valuation
- Sector standard valuation
- Discounted cashflow
- P & L valuation
- Assets valuation.

These different methods can produce very different valuations; therefore, it is usual to use more than one method to arrive at a valuation.

Let's take a look at them in more detail.

Entry cost valuation

The alternative to buying an existing business is to create a new one or add the extra capability to an existing business.

The entry cost valuation calculates what it would cost to get to the same point as the business being valued. It is likely to include estimates of the following:

- Purchasing assets
- Researching, developing and patenting products and services
- Establishing operating systems
- Recruiting and training employees
- Developing and trade marking brands
- Developing sales and marketing collateral
- Building a similar sized customer base.

This valuation method is likely to be used if the business under consideration has yet to achieve a level of success that would make one of the other methods more appropriate.

It may also be used as a check against one of the other valuation methods.

To maximise this valuation, make sure you fully document all expenditure and document the hours worked by key personnel at an appropriate rate.

Time is a huge factor in establishing a business and most owners work a significant amount of time outside of normal hours that is never credited.

Industry standard valuation

Some industry sectors tend to value acquisitions according to a general formula that defines what the business might be worth to them. For example, valuations might be dependent on the number of customers, contracts or outlets.

An accountancy practice tends to be valued at 0.8 – 1.2 times gross recurring fees. This reflects the nature of accountancy fees as regularly recurring and the relatively high resistance to changing accountants.

Discounted Cashflow valuation

This valuation method tends to be used for predictable businesses such as a publisher with established titles or a utility firm, especially in a monopoly situation such as a water supplier.

Future cashflow is estimated and then discounted on the basis that inflation erodes the value of future revenues against those received today. The discount rate applied is based on the cost of capital and usually includes an adjustment to reflect the risk of the cash flow projections.

P & L Valuation

When someone buys a business they are buying the potential to earn profits in the future. The extent of future profits depends on the forecasted future turnover and the profitability.

P & L valuations tend to use either a multiple of annual net profit or a proportion of annual turnover.

The choice of which and the multiplying factor applied will depend on the industry sector.

A business increases in value as it grows as long as it maintains its profitability.

The rate of growth experienced by the business is an important additional factor to impress on a potential purchaser.

If growth begins to slow, it can have a detrimental impact on the valuation of the business. A business that has been at the same turnover level for several years is likely to have a lower valuation than a business that has shown steady growth over the preceding years, yet has only just achieved a similar level of turnover. This reflects its growth trajectory and the expectation that it will soon out-perform the first company.

Assets Valuation

Net Assets Valuation is the figure often taken to mean the Net Worth of a business, i.e. the sum of assets, both tangible and intangible, less liabilities. Liabilities include any loans that have to be repaid.

Many prospective investors will be reluctant to pay more than this for a business, because this is the amount of money that could be realised if necessary.

In the industrial era the ability to generate turnover and profits could be reasonably measured by a company's tangible assets. Businesses that still tend to be valued according to tangible assets include: shipping, manufacturing and property-based businesses.

However, it is now more common for businesses to have good turnover and profitability without the need for a large tangible asset base.

Many businesses also have intangible assets and where possible the value of these should be estimated and included in the balance sheet. Valuing intangible assets can be difficult and may be disputed by potential purchasers.

The most obvious intangible asset is the company brand or product brand names. For a relatively small company the brand name can still represent significant value for a potential purchaser.

Intangible assets include:

- Long-term contracts for supply
- A license or distributorship for a product
- Patents, trademarks and registered designs
- Company and product brand names
- Key expertise or relationships
- Goodwill.

The value of a contract is relatively easy to calculate. The value of a license or distributorship can also be estimated for its duration.

The value of protecting a market via patents, trademarks and registered designs is more difficult to calculate, but a valuation can be roughly estimated over the life of the protection.

One way to measure the value of a brand name or product name may be to consider conversion rates. The brand name may be partly responsible for a better than typical conversion rate for customer acquisition.

The effect of this may be to reduce the cost of customer acquisition and improve growth and profitability. Although the extent of the effect would have to be validated, once done so the business valuation can be calculated with and without the impact of the brand and enable a value to be placed against the brand.

Asset valuations are broadly the sum of assets, both tangible and intangible, less liabilities, but there is an additional element that is much more difficult to quantify and normally referred to as 'goodwill'.

Goodwill is effectively the difference between the purchase price of a business and the value of the acquired assets, both tangible and intangible, less liabilities.

Goodwill reflects the intangible assets that would not be included in a valuation of its net assets in the Balance Sheet, but would in part be responsible for the turnover and profits of the business.

The International Financial Reporting Standards, which are applicable to all quoted companies, defines goodwill as "...*a payment made by the acquirer in anticipation of future economic benefits from assets that are not capable of being individually identified and separately recognised*" (IFRS 3 paragraph 52).

However, goodwill has in the past exceeded half the purchase price of a business, which is the reason why the regulations have now been tightened. There is a concern that shareholders of the purchasing company could be defrauded by the company's management. The assumption being that the decision makers may somehow have an interest in the company being acquired.

As a result, the nature of goodwill is now expected to be more fully disclosed, as dictated by IFRS 3 paragraph 66h: "...*a description of each intangible asset that was not recognised separately from goodwill and an explanation of why the intangible asset's fair value could not be measured reliably...*"

To achieve the best asset valuation of your business make sure you maximise the value of your intangible assets and that means registering them to protect them from being copied or used by other businesses.

From the outset, you will be pumping cash into your brand so it is crazy not to make sure this is a brand name that will be valuable in the longer-term. Your own name or initials may not be the best choice.

Once you've chosen your company brand and any product or service brand names make sure you get them registered immediately.

Also consider patents for any products and consider registering designs that you are promoting even if they are not assigned to a specific product. For example, the 'heart of business success' used in this book is a registered design. It could be used on a book jacket, diary, calendar, mouse mat or a tee shirt - the important point is that it is registered and therefore of more value.

If you don't register before you begin promoting a possible patent or registered design it may no longer be possible to register it. Once it's in the public domain it may not be possible for the Intellectual Property Office to be able to validate you or your company as the original source.

Applying for a patent or registered design will introduce a delay in your ability to use it, hence make sure you organise it as soon as you can. You don't want to commit funds to your capacity if it would be less effective without the registration of a patent or design.

It only costs a few hundred pounds to register trademarks, patents and designs, but it can make a significant difference to your business valuation. If your business valuation is based on your ability to trade in a global market don't forget that it will cost a lot more and take longer to protect your rights across all the different territories.

Deciding when to exit

You're unlikely to get the best valuation for your business if you have to sell when you haven't planned to exit.

If you part-own your business or someone else has taken an equity stake in return for a share of your business you will have to agree an exit strategy and timeframe.

Your partnership is more likely to be successful if you work towards the same exit plan.

Knowing the likely exit parameters in advance means you can plan to strengthen your balance sheet and maximise the valuation of the business at that point.

When somebody buys your business, they are buying its potential to earn profits in the future. Even if you maximise the value of your assets and especially your intangible assets, for most businesses the highest valuation is likely to be the P & L Valuation.

To maximise the P & L Valuation you will need to maximise two elements:

1. Growth in the preceding years

2. Profitability.

This is the Exit Dilemma, because during periods of strong growth your focus should be on cash management at the expense of profit to ensure that you neither run out of cash nor stall before you've reached the next Stability Step.

Yet during periods of stability when your focus can shift to maximising profit, you will be more limited in growth.

This suggests to us that there is only one point on the 'S' curve where you should aim to sell for maximum valuation. It is the point where you approach a Stability Step and profits can be maximised, but you still show a recent history of strong growth.

As you move along the plateau of a Stability Step your business valuation is unlikely to increase, but may actually decline because you will not be showing a recent history of growth.

Although this limits your flexibility as to when you can get the best valuation for your business, in a way it can be beneficial because it focuses you to a specific point to exit. So, it helps you to make the Exit Dilemma Decision.

There is still plenty of choice, because it doesn't tell you which of the various Stability Steps would be the right point for your exit.

When you move onto a Stability Step and don't yet intend to exit, you can use the period of stability to build your asset base. This should enable you to improve your future profitability and increase the asset valuation of the business.

I frequently hear owners of small businesses discussing how to minimise their corporation tax liability by reducing profits. If you don't plan to exit for a while, it makes sense to reduce your corporation tax liability by investing in your asset base, but if you're within a few years of exit it may be more beneficial to record good and growing profitability and take the tax hit in order to maximise the valuation of your business.

When you decide to exit, whoever takes over the business will have to make their exit choice further up the ambition ladder.

Let's consider a capacity-driven business, such as a restaurant or a children's nursery, phase one might be to grow it quickly to maximum capacity and possibly sell. It will show good growth in preceding years and its best profitability as it approaches maximum utilisation.

Phase two might be to capitalise on the brand name and your experience and open a chain of five outlets each with an individual manager and all within a reasonable geographic area that would enable you to manage the whole business.

In the second phase you will take advantage of what you've already achieved, borrowed against that achievement and leveraged the effort of other people.

The return on the investment of your time and money is likely to be much greater than for a single outlet.

If you exit too early, you may not yet have achieved a better return on the effort you've put in than you would have done working for someone else over the same period.

On the other hand, if you exit too late, you may get bored and find your lack of attention has allowed growth to slow and the valuation to be reduced.

The Delegation Dilemma

There is a further issue that can reduce the valuation of a business and I refer to it as the Delegation Dilemma.

If the business is still relatively small, there is more likely to be an emotional attachment between the present business owner and any valuable clients or key employees. So, a potential purchaser of the business will be concerned that these valuable customers or key employees may not be retained after acquisition. Yet these valuable customers and the expertise that resides within these key employees form a substantial part of the value being purchased, i.e. its ability to earn profits in the future.

Most small business owners believe they should endeavour to maintain their personal relationships with valuable clients and key employees. And generally this may well help to improve client and employee retention, but it may also make the transition to a new owner more precarious and hence reduce the value of the business.

The delegation dilemma refers to the level of involvement that a business owner has in the business. If the business owner stays close to customers and employees to enhance motivation and retention the business owner may appear to be too critical for a potential buyer to proceed. Yet if the owner doesn't keep close to what's going on there is a real threat that the business may deviate and become less effective and grow more slowly.

As a business grows, the relationship between the current owner and clients or employees will inevitably diminish which will reduce the risk for a purchaser and so can actually increase its value.

This is an example of the sort of balance required when aiming to grow a business to the point where someone else is prepared to acquire it.

One way to help overcome the delegation dilemma is to use long-term contracts to tie-in key customers and employees. But this is a 'barrier' strategy rather than a 'benefit' strategy, i.e. using a stick rather than a carrot. I always prefer to go for a benefit strategy because barrier strategies can lead you into a false sense of security.

In today's global market, customers and employees have more choice and they will be more inclined towards a business using 'benefit' strategies rather than 'barrier' strategies.

The reality is that most barrier strategies will only delay the inevitable, but will usually cause negative feeling and may unnecessarily damage your brand. Consider mortgage providers issuing contracts with redemption clauses, requiring you to pay a fee to switch providers.

A better way to overcome the Delegation Dilemma is to avoid having to rely on a few key customers and a few key employees.

The best way to avoid a reliance on a few key customers is to expand your customer base.

The best way to avoid a reliance on a few key people is to establish good process and systemise all activities. Whenever you have a process that you will need to do more than once, you should document and systemise it.

Systems

Systems can improve efficiency and reduce the level of capacity required to service the same number of customers.

Systems make it easier to maintain and monitor standards as your business expands. When people are absent, systems make it easier for others to cover their work and maintain customer service. Imagine how you would feel if you contacted a business with a query about your order only to be told that the person dealing with it is away for two weeks and would you call back when they return.

Systems also help to ensure the business runs smoothly in your absence and therefore, will help to make the business more attractive to prospective buyers.

Systems enable the business to operate according to the present requirements of your business and your customer's present requirements. This means that the better your systems the more you are liberated to be creative and work 'on' your business rather than 'in' it and to consider your customer's future requirements.

If your systems are not sufficient, you will be continually drawn into the day-to-day activities. The better your systems the more likely you are to stay ahead of the competition.

Systems are essential to be able to expand your business and enable you to scale it more quickly.

It's never too early to develop your systems as they will have an immediate effect on efficiency and customer service.

One of my clients asked me to help them specify a computerised system for the business because the owner felt that he didn't have sufficient control over what his employees were doing. He wanted it in place before he expanded his work force.

I spent some time working through their manual processes and was able to specify a data base system to streamline their work. Some of the existing employees were initially reluctant to help, probably because they were apprehensive about something new and unknown.

Once the system was installed and had been operating for a few months, the owner called me with some remarkable feedback.

He had become concerned that the business was declining because people didn't seem to be as busy, but when he checked the figures he found that they were doing twice as much as the previous year, but without the stress.

The level of customer dissatisfaction had reduced because everyone could immediately check any customer order from their own computer without having to search for a file.

He also mentioned that he had chosen not to take on an extra person that he had been planning to recruit because the capacity of the existing employees was now sufficient.

This meant that the system had paid for itself within a matter of months.

The system had delivered the following benefits:

- Improved the efficiency and profitability of the business
- Improved service levels
- Reduced the reliance on key employees
- Made it easier to train new employees
- Become an asset that increased the value of the business.

It's important to be able to show to a prospective purchaser that your business is properly systemised. It will give them confidence that the business will continue to work efficiently and grow under new ownership and may encourage them to select your business over an alternative.

Let's return now to the Exit Dilemma with an example.

One of my clients was a company run by two partners and they had spent five years and a huge amount of effort building their business and its client base, but it was beginning to take its toll on their relationship.

They had stopped enjoying the business, they didn't like the effect it was having on their friendship and reluctantly they'd decided to sell. They wanted me to help them arrive at a business valuation and construct a prospectus for the sale of their business.

I showed them the calculations of business valuation and explained that the rule of 80:20 seemed to be applicable. They had put in 80% of the effort required to achieve success, but had so far only achieved 20% of the likely valuation.

Whilst they would probably get their cash investment back, they would be unlikely to receive any reward for their considerable effort and achievement so far. In effect, they would have been better off working for someone else and not having all the stress of running a business and employing people.

We worked through the situation and agreed that the business could now afford to employ a manager to run it on a day-to-day basis and grow it according to the business plan we had previously developed. They had already invested in systems to ensure the business could run efficiently without their involvement.

Employing a Business Manager meant that they could work 'on' the business rather than 'in' it and this would reduce the pressure on their friendship.

Within a few years the business would be in a far better position to sell for a more appropriate valuation to reward them for their efforts.

So, just as in the Entry Catch-22 you need to calculate the first Stability Step and minimise the cash required to get you there; for the Exit Catch-22, you also need to calculate a Stability Step, but this time to maximise the cash you walk away with.

As far as possible, decide in advance your Ambition Aim and Time Target for exit and plan how you will achieve it.

Ambition Aims

Here are some examples of Ambition Aims that may drive your exit plan. In each case you'll notice there's a Time Target. Only when the extent of your ambition is coupled with a Time Target can you define a Growth Gradient and calculate the finance required to deliver it.

If you don't feel able to fund, or comfortable with the level of cash that you would need to invest, you'll have to reduce your Ambition Aim or extend your Time Target in order to reduce your Growth Gradient.

- **Turnover:** grow annual revenues to £3m within 5 years – Revenues are driven by the numbers and types of customers you can acquire. Calculate the capacity required to service your growing customer numbers. Capacity follows Customers.

- **Market share:** grow market share to 5% within 5 years – Market share can be defined by customer numbers or revenues or both. Calculate the capacity required to service your growing customer numbers. Capacity follows Customers.

- **Utilisation:** grow demand to 85% occupancy within 3 years – This relates to accommodating customers in a building with a fixed capacity, e.g. recording studio, treatment rooms for a beauty salon or physiotherapy practice. Maximising utilisation will drive your customer acquisition strategy. Customers follow Capacity.

- **Resources:** grow resource numbers to 100 within 5 years, e.g. number of business advisors or financial advisors. Calculate the numbers of customers required to match your growing capacity. Customers follow Capacity.

- **Outlets:** grow the number of outlets to 10 within 5 years – This type of capacity target will define your market share target and the proximity of outlets to each other. Customers and Capacity must balance.

- **Profit:** grow profit to £500k within 5 years. For a service-based business, profit is enhanced when capacity is fully utilised. For a product-based business, better profitability may be achieved by buying in bulk, but this may require more cash, which may reduce profits. Customers and Capacity must balance.

- **Business valuation:** grow the valuation of the business to £5m within 10 years – A business is only ever worth what someone is prepared to pay for it. This Ambition Aim is also the main subject of this book, but it will need to be expanded to indicate exactly how you expect to achieve the valuation. Business valuation tends to increase with turnover, growth history and profitability. Customers and Capacity must balance.

Beware of the 'law of unintended consequences', which states that any purposeful action will produce some unintended consequences.

A classic example occurs when a salesperson is offered a bonus related to a sales target and given the authority to offer discounts. The business may find its margins eroded as the sales person is tempted to offer discounts to secure orders.

When establishing your Ambition Aim it is a good idea to merge more than one of the examples listed above. For example, if you set a turnover or market share aim, it would be wise to include a profit aim alongside it.

Overcoming the Exit Catch-22 – Financing ambition

We've already seen the importance of cash to facilitate your growth and achieve your ambition. We've also looked at how to calculate the amount of finance you need for the Growth Gradient that will deliver your Ambition Aim within your Time Target.

Yet as soon as you try to obtain that funding the Exit Catch-22 means you need even more just to finance it.

The Exit Catch-22 is defined as follows:

Your desired exit valuation requires a level of funding – yet the level of funding increases the exit valuation you require.

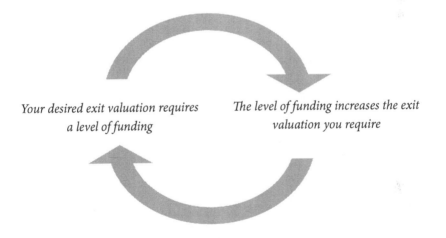

Your desired exit valuation requires a level of funding

The level of funding increases the exit valuation you require

There are 3 primary options for business finance:

1. Equity Finance – funds in exchange for a share of the company

2. Debt Finance – overdrafts and loans

3. Asset Finance – leasing or hire-purchase, factoring or invoice discounting.

There are also several alternative options that can work for particular businesses and we shall come onto those later.

First, let's run through the primary options:

Equity Finance

Equity Finance is desired by many owners of small businesses because they don't need to put up security, which would be the case for a bank loan and they usually haven't realised the full consequences of the Exit Catch-22.

There are several levels of Equity Finance beginning with Angel Finance.

A Business Angel will typically help to grow a young business in return for a relatively high equity stake to reflect the risk.

Once a business has a proven proposition and is ready to scale, it often needs another major injection of capital. This is usually referred to as venture finance and is more likely to be a private equity firm or venture capital company.

Investors, whether they are Angels or Venture Capitalists, will be most attracted by business opportunities that are able to demonstrate strong scalability.

There are three key requirements for scalability:

- The market is strong and sufficiently large

- The business proposition is competitive

- The profit as a percentage of sales increases as the business grows.

The profit percentage will increase as the business scales if the incremental cost of adding new customers declines.

Most businesses have some fixed costs that change little as the business grows, such as the costs of the head office and the Managing Director's salary.

The impact of these fixed overhead costs reduces as the business grows and acquires more customers.

It can cost a great deal to develop a new product and as the business grows these costs can be amortised across more and more customers.

Variable costs are the costs a business incurs only when it makes a sale, for example the cost of a product being traded. The cost of sale can also reduce as a business grows, for example it can buy in larger quantities to get better prices from suppliers.

All of these can be referred to as 'economy of scale', but for a truly scalable business, investors are looking for something more.

Consider the case of a software developer; once a new application has been developed the cost of selling the software to each new customer becomes marginal.

The cost of sale is limited to packaging and distribution. With many software applications now being downloaded via the Internet, the costs of packaging can be zero. The costs of distribution may still include the credit card transaction charges and any commissions paid to the download site.

In this example, the most significant expense is likely to be one of promotion. As long as customers have a clear need and are willing to find a solution to that need via the Internet even the costs of promotion can be relatively low-cost.

The Internet offers a great opportunity for very scalable businesses because it is possible to both sell and deliver via the Internet.

So, as long as the software has wide appeal and minimal competition, it will have good scalability because it will clearly have the opportunity for the profit percentage to continue to rise the more it sells.

Unfortunately, there is usually a point where the incremental cost of adding new customers stops declining because the business has reached a certain market share; and to gain a larger share it would have to spend proportionately more, i.e. the cost of acquisition starts rising.

Just because the opportunity is scalable, doesn't mean the market is large enough to recoup the investment and then make large profits. So, although investors search for scalable businesses, they have to be realistic about the extent of that scalability.

So, how scalable is your business and therefore how attractive is the opportunity to an investor?

- How big is the market?

- To what extent is your proposition competitive and hence, what market share would it be reasonable to target?

- Will the profit percentage increase as the business scales? Are you able to demonstrate that for every new customer you add, the cost associated with adding each new customer is lower?

It is sometimes possible to add systems that will enable you to service or process customers more efficiently. For example, one of my clients delivers a service largely via the Internet. They have just secured second stage funding and one of the key requirements for the funding is to develop systems to dramatically reduce the time taken to service customers. This will have a huge impact on efficiency and the cost-of-sale, which will enable the business to scale without the need to recruit and train additional capacity at the current rate.

A common dilemma is how ambitious you should be when pitching for investment. Many people don't want to appear ridiculously ambitious and tend to understate the level of scalability of their business opportunity.

Whereas, most investors want to see just how scalable the opportunity could be; their favourite word is 'stretch'. Investors often like to work with you on your business opportunity to explore just how far it could potentially stretch.

This doesn't mean that they want to remain with the business all the way, but they know the exit valuation will be higher the more potential there is still available.

Whether or not you can attract Equity Finance will often come down to how scalable it is. So, if the proposition is not particularly scalable or you're not sufficiently ambitious, you may find it difficult to attract professional equity investment.

If your business is scalable and you are hoping to attract a professional investor, remember that once an investor has put funds into your business those funds are tied up for the foreseeable future. This means they are no longer available to invest in an alternative opportunity that may be presented to the investor.

You need to present the strongest proposal possible and keep as many potential investors interested as you can because the way to overcome the Exit Catch-22 is to attract the right investor.

As we discussed in Part 1, the Exit Catch-22 normally means that you have to get on a steeper growth gradient to compensate for the relinquished equity, but the steeper growth gradient requires more funding, so you have to give up even more equity.

Imagine if you were able to attract an investor with existing access to new customers for your product or service. It would be in the interest of the investor to broker connections for you.

The way to overcome the Exit Catch-22 is to select an investor that will bring expertise and contacts to help you achieve a steeper growth gradient without the need for additional funding and without having to give up any more equity.

For businesses that are unlikely to scale to any great extent – and most will be in this position – it may be difficult to attract Equity Finance in the usual way.

Most businesses will be in this position. Yet this does not mean that you can't get somebody to invest in your business.

An alternative might be to approach a company already operating within your target market that may be prepared to diversify in preparation for expansion.

The kind of company you're after is likely to be operating within the same target market as you, but offering a complementary product or service or even a similar service at a different level.

Buying a share in your business would give them exposure to your area of expertise. It would provide them with a good insight into your field and enable them to decide whether to integrate the two businesses at a later date.

The potential purchaser would benefit from your efforts in growing the business and both businesses could help each other as partners.

In this way, you will potentially benefit from the partnership by more than just the investment of funds.

This will help achieve a steeper growth gradient than just finding someone to invest in your business and again enable you to overcome the Exit Catch-22

You could even negotiate a reciprocal shareholding in the other company albeit at a smaller percentage. This would cement the partnership and encourage you to support them where you're able.

If this is an appropriate route for you, local networking may be a good way to become acquainted with possible business partners.

You will still need a thorough business plan and a professional pitch to secure Equity Finance in this way.

Part 3 covers planning for success in detail and at the end of Part 3 there is also a section on pitching to an investor.

Debt Finance

Usually provided by banks, Debt Finance refers to loans and overdrafts and can be surprisingly difficult for a small business to obtain. The issue is one of risk because the bank's business model is to charge interest on the outstanding loan.

Lenders don't benefit from capital growth, so they rely on the loan and interest being repaid in full.

This means they try to limit risk and bank lending tends to be conservative.

Unless a loan is relatively small, most banks would normally require you to underwrite the loan by putting up security – usually in the form of property.

Whilst this might be frustrating for the business owner, it simply reflects the risk versus reward in the interest business model offered by lenders.

Lenders will need a thorough business plan showing exactly how you intend to use the loan to check it is destined for business development.

As I write this we are in the first few weeks of 2009 and in the midst of the credit crunch. The daily news is full of more problems for the banks and it's increasingly difficult for businesses to obtain a loan, which is adding to the deepening recession.

Having said that, I've just taken a phone call from a very pleased client of mine letting me know that the plan we put together has been accepted by the bank and they've agreed an unsecured loan. OK, it wasn't a large loan, but even so, it proves that if you put a persuasive plan together you can obtain finance even in the most difficult times.

The Government may underwrite a significant proportion of a bank loan for a small business where the owners are unable to put up security.

Government schemes work on the basis that the bank conducts its normal risk assessment process. Where the bank would otherwise lend but for lack of security feels unable, the Government will step in to underwrite up to seventy five percent of it.

This policy is designed to cultivate small businesses, create employment and boost the economy and ultimately future tax revenues.

The best strategy for Debt Finance is to reduce the amount of loan by as much as possible using some of the other techniques and then to show how easily you would be able to service the debt.

Make sure you include the schedule of loan repayments and interest payments in your projections, which of course increases the amount you need to borrow.

Also include some contingency because the banks get very nervous if you go back after a few months and tell them you should have asked for more.

In many cases the bank may have lent more if originally requested but asking for it subsequently, often meets with rejection.

Debt Finance is almost the opposite of Equity Finance and you're more likely to get a loan if you don't show too great a stretch. Usually, the greater the stretch, i.e. the steeper the growth gradient, the greater the risk will be perceived to be.

With Debt Finance you're more likely to obtain an overdraft or a bank loan if you show that you would be able to repay the debt with minimal risk.

Asset Finance

If lending can be secured against capital equipment it is referred to as Asset Finance. A down-payment is usually required as the finance company will want to be able to recoup the funds by selling the equipment second hand in the event of default. The better the second hand value of an asset the lower the down-payment requested.

It may also be possible to obtain Asset Finance against an intangible asset, such as a contract that has been won. This would enable a business to begin working on the contract in advance. The contract would have to be very secure, so the finance company would consider it more favourably if it were issued by a Government department, Local Authority or major corporation.

Factoring and Invoice Discounting

The invoices that have been issued by a company and not yet paid by the customer are also considered to be assets. Factoring and Invoice Discounting is where you sell your invoices for an agreed percentage, so you get paid quickly and the Factoring Company collects the money from your customers when it falls due.

This can be a useful way to fund your trading cashflow as you grow, although it doesn't provide the initial investment kick that a lump sum will. This is likely to mean you have to grow more slowly.

If a customer doesn't pay the invoice within a reasonable term, the finance company will normally charge the invoice back to the company. So, the business still shoulders the risk and can not use it as an alternative to the normal credit checking procedures. The finance company will also be watching for bogus invoices being issued to help massage cash flow.

Alternative Finance Options

Here are some alternative ways that you can finance your business growth.

You may be able to implement several of these options or think of some other ideas. Alternative options may not be able to entirely replace the need for a loan or equity finance, but they may reduce the extent of primary funding required and help to overcome the Exit Catch-22.

Financing against debit or credit card transactions

An alternative to raising finance against invoices is now available to businesses where a reasonable number of transactions are made via debit and credit cards.

The finance company will provide a lump sum against future card transactions. They will then collect a fixed proportion of all future card transactions.

The system is flexible as there is no fixed amount to be collected each month and there is no fixed term to the finance. More is collected in a good month and less in a poor month – this makes it easier to manage your cash flow.

To qualify, the business needs to provide several months of debit or credit card trading history. You may have to change the service provider you use to process card transactions to one nominated by the finance company.

Supplier Finance

Suppliers will sometimes offer interest-free credit for a period. This can be funded either from their own reserves or by arrangement with an Asset Finance company.

For example, the computer on which I'm compiling this book was one of several purchased with credit arranged through the manufacturer, but provided by an independent finance company. A nominal arrangement fee was charged and then no payments were due for a period of one year. After that we had the choice of paying the balance in full or paying monthly for a further three years. We chose to pay the full amount after one year because the interest charges for the next three years were somewhat onerous.

These kinds of arrangements may be useful as long as you're clear about the terms. Although the finance company should remind you when you need to make payment in full to avoid incurring further interest payments, it makes sense to schedule your own reminder.

Now, the concept I really want to cover under Supplier Finance is that of shared risk and reward.

Perhaps the best way to introduce this is with an example. One of my clients needed to develop some software to help service their customers more efficiently.

In common with many software projects there was a real possibility of 'specification creep', meaning the client would extend the requirements as the project progressed.

This can be difficult for both the client and the supplier when it comes to fair pricing. The supplier could add a high percentage of contingency within the price and then agree to accept minor amendments to the specification within the agreed price. Alternatively, the supplier could make additional charges for every amendment.

It is not uncommon for the final price of software to spiral way beyond the original estimate and take much longer than expected. If disagreements occur it becomes increasingly difficult for the client to switch suppliers because too much has already been committed. If they simply stop, the software may never be properly fit for purpose.

My client has negotiated an alternative solution to this type of situation. The supplier has initially been paid a fixed fee, which is considerably lower than the likely commercial value of the software development time. The agreement is then for my client to pay the supplier commission on sales made using the software.

The supplier takes the risk that my client will be successful and will continue to pay commissions. The more successful my client becomes the more revenue the software supplier continues to earn. Furthermore, they've agreed that no commission becomes due until the equivalent of the original fixed fee has been reached.

- The advantage to my client is that the upfront investment is much reduced

- The advantage to the supplier is that the total return on the development could be much increased

- The advantage to both of them is that they save the time and effort normally taken up with compiling and negotiating a detailed specification; not only at the outset, but also for every subsequent amendment.

This kind of arrangement enables more efficient use of resources for both parties and reduces the scope for disputes.

In this spirit of shared risk and reward, my client was able to reduce the amount of external funding required.

This kind of supplier finance can also be used for product development.

Customer Finance

If your business develops a product or undertakes a project on behalf of a customer you will incur costs that are directly attributable to the project. Not only will this impact your cashflow, but there is always a risk that your customer will run into financial difficulties and not be able to pay your invoices when they fall due.

The best approach is to ask for an advance payment and then aim for each project to be cash positive all the way through by asking for regular payments against scheduled work completed.

If customers are reluctant to provide advance payments, it usually indicates a lack of trust or liquidity, either way there will be implications that you need to address.

If you look at each new project as an opportunity to finance your growth, it will create the right focus for both winning the project and helping to achieve your ambition. Asking for the advance payments that make it all possible just becomes a necessary part of the process.

Government Grants

Governments aim to support small businesses with grants; however, most of these require an element of matched funds. This means that you will still need access to other funding to match the grant.

There are different types of grant funds usually established to encourage the achievement of specific Government objectives, such as improving the skill base through training and apprenticeships, increasing energy efficiency or encouraging the development of new technology.

To take advantage of a Government grant you need to find one that is a good fit with your own objectives. Try not to get distracted from your primary focus just to get access to a grant. I've seen people spend a lot of time and get very frustrated trying to find a route through to a Government grant.

The Government has its agenda and you have yours – if they coincide, that's great, but otherwise you'll have to look for an alternative source of funding.

Sponsorship

We're all familiar with sponsorship – take a look at any sporting event. But sponsorship doesn't have to be restricted to sport and expeditions, it can work for certain businesses as well.

Can you use sponsorship to fund or part-fund some of your promotional activity?

You have to convince a potential sponsor that you can publicise their brand to a reasonable number of their target audience in a positive manner.

For the company being sponsored, it's another form of funding. For the sponsor, it's another form of promotional activity and should be judged in terms of its relative return-on-investment compared with alternatives.

If you want a slice of a sponsor's marketing budget you have to show them why this opportunity has the potential to out-perform other promotional options.

What can you do to increase the size of the audience and likely conversion rate to make it more attractive to a sponsor? Perhaps you can get a publication to agree in advance that they will cover the event and feature you.

You could identify a publication that targets a specific audience on a national basis or you could target a wider audience, but only on a local basis through a local paper. Obtain the typical circulation figures for the publication and include it in your pitch to sponsors.

Offer sponsors more than one option at different levels, perhaps in terms of the size or position of their logo in advertisements, banners, printed material and press releases.

It can help if you already have a relationship with a potential sponsor before you have to approach them for money. Look at your existing customers or suppliers first. If you think sponsorship might work for your business, try to plan ahead and begin creating relationships as early as possible. You may even select a supplier for your normal requirements with future sponsorship in mind.

By the way, a sponsor doesn't have to be the bigger party. For example, if you're intending to participate in a trade show, perhaps you can find smaller companies with complementary products that are not planning to have a stand. You could offer them some promotional space and off-set some of your costs. They're paying for visibility on the back of your efforts – that's sponsorship.

After the event, you should try to get some feedback on how successful the event was for the sponsor. This may be invaluable when you next have an opportunity for sponsorship.

Partnership or Joint Venture

Is there an opportunity to share costs with another company, perhaps for product development, capacity or customer acquisition?

Let's look at each of these briefly.

Product development

Developing products and services can require substantial finance and it may be possible to share the costs with partners. The main issue is whether each partner can operate in a distinct market or geography that limits the extent of competitive friction.

The term 'White Label' refers to a product or service produced by one company and then rebranded and marketed by other companies. The term originates from the record industry where DJs would remove the label on a vinyl record to prevent other DJs from seeing the details of the artist and publisher.

You may be able to find a producer of a product or service prepared to 'white label' it enabling you to market it to your customer base until you have the means to develop your own.

Alternatively, you may want to produce and offer a 'white labelled' product or service to others and even get them to contribute towards the development costs.

Capacity

If your current need for an asset or resource would not be sufficient to fully utilise it, perhaps you can share with a similar but non-competing local company.

Where you are able to fully utilise an employee with a particular skill, but don't have the demand to employ a second person with the same skill, you will need cover in times of absence due to holidays and illness. It may be possible to agree a reciprocal arrangement of covering absences with a company that has similar issues. Ideally the partner will provide a very similar service but not in competition with you.

Customer acquisition

When businesses overlap in terms of the audience they target but not the product or service they provide there are many opportunities to combine forces and promote more efficiently. Sometimes, it can even be more effective because the partners can offer a more complete package to the customer.

Collaboration may be in the form of a piece of direct mail, a stand at a trade show or running a seminar.

There are some risks to consider, like the effect on your brand if the partner doesn't perform well. So it's important to choose your partners wisely. Try to get to know them before you commit and avoid any contracts that bind you into an exclusive arrangement.

If you don't already know the company, ask them for a few customer references and speak to them. Their customers will quickly inform you of the satisfaction levels they're currently achieving.

Managing Cashflow

This book has shown that cashflow is the life blood of a business and without which it will fail. If you keep the heart model in balance as you grow you should be able to plan to receive more cash from customers than you outlay to acquire them and service them.

When a business starts or begins any new growth phase it will require access to a lump sum of cash and eventually this is planned to be recovered by increased revenues – as depicted by the 'hockey stick' growth profile for cumulative cash.

We've already discussed the implication on cash versus profit of holding stock or leasing rather than buying capital items, so we don't need to repeat those discussions here.

However, there are a number of other techniques that can reduce your trading cash requirement and may actually make it possible to grow using a reduced level of cash investment.

These techniques should be embedded in your process and systems to ensure cashflow is always a priority throughout the business. This helps to ensure that you don't have to spend hours on the tedious task of managing your cashflow when you could be working on more exciting business development opportunities.

Let's look at a few of these simple techniques to improve your cashflow.

Customers

Always ensure invoices are issued as soon as it is appropriate. Any delay in issuing the invoice not only translates to the same delay before it falls due for payment, but it also sends a message to the customer that prompt payment is not a priority for you. This could mean that they agree to pay another supplier's invoice in preference to yours.

Some people feel awkward about the whole money side of business. I can remember on several occasions having to ask a small supplier to send me an invoice. One of them told me how much she loved working with her customers, but found the whole invoicing and payment side of the business to be slightly distasteful.

This is a mindset and a good way to overcome it is to think of money as merely a means of exchange. Bartering is the exchange of products or services and money enables that exchange to extend beyond the two parties involved in the immediate transaction. If the person needing your products or services cannot provide you with something you need, paying you with money enables you to get whatever you need elsewhere.

So, the actual agreement between you and the customer occurred when you offered a quotation or agreed a price and they accepted it. The best time for negotiation is before you even begin work. This is recognised and reflected in commercial law.

If you think of payment in this way, it should be much easier to send an invoice to a customer as soon as you've delivered the pre-agreed product or service.

There is another very good reason for being prompt with your invoicing. If you're sometimes lax with your invoicing and then you become prompt, it may be perceived by the customer as a sign of cashflow problems.

Customers get nervous about suppliers that are struggling and it may encourage a customer to switch supplier.

The solution is to set the standard from the very first invoice issued to a new customer and they will simply perceive you as being professional.

If you offer credit terms to customers it makes good sense to keep the period of credit short, for example 7 days or 14 days rather than 30 days. Once the due date is passed have an automatic system of reminders for chasing payment regularly until payment has been received. When it comes to money people tend to respond to those who chase hardest.

Don't forget to conduct a credit check on new customers and if they have a poor rating ask for payment in advance or cash-on-delivery. This is always important and even more so during an economic downturn as the risk of default increases.

If you have existing customers who consistently pay late, consider changing the terms to cash-on-delivery

If your business provides services to customers on a project basis, e.g. architect, builder, software developer, web site developer, graphic designer, it is often possible to obtain an advance payment. This can have a significant impact on your cashflow.

When I model a business I include the likely profile of customer payment and this can show the impact on cumulative cash of different payment profiles. My clients are often surprised by the impact it can have.

Shortening payment terms and embedding procedures to encourage prompt payment can significantly reduce the cash requirement or enable you to grow faster with the same cash investment.

Suppliers

Don't always focus on the lowest price when choosing suppliers. The lowest price may be appropriate when you're on a Stability Step and going for profit. But when you're growing and focussing on cash, more flexible payment terms may be more important.

The same consideration can be applied for suppliers that offer a discount for early payment.

Try to use all the credit period offered by your suppliers. This is much easier if you use an automatic payment transfer so you can set up a payment as soon as an invoice is received, but timed to make full use of the credit period.

Try to extend supplier credit terms where possible.

If the timing of a purchase can affect when you have to pay, work out when to make purchases for maximum credit. Of course, if you need something sooner in order to fulfil customer orders any delay may slow the receipt of cash and negate any advantage.

Tax

The VAT period for most businesses is quarterly and payment is due by the end of the month following the quarter. If you have stock purchases or capital items such as vehicles, equipment and computers, where you will be claiming the VAT back, it makes good sense to buy them at the end of the quarter.

This means your VAT account will be credited in the shortest time reducing the amount you owe or even generating a credit.

Again, there may be other more significant factors that outweigh this benefit, for example, you may not want to delay servicing a customer just so that you can delay a purchase. Or bring a purchase forward to time it with the end of a VAT quarter when you're unlikely to have the cash to pay for it when the invoice falls due.

Currency

Exchange rate planning may be required if you price your work in a currency that is different from the currency in which you incur a large proportion of costs.

A client of mine buys his products in Euros yet sells mainly in UK Sterling and recently the pound has weakened substantially against the Euro, which has been depressing his margins.

The obvious approach is to pass on part of the cost increase to customers. Whether this is possible depends on a number of factors:

- Is the customer's willingness to buy the product sensitive to price?

- Are any of the alternative suppliers sourcing equivalent products in a currency that would give them a competitive advantage?

- Are there contracts in place that fix the price for an agreed period?

Exchange rate variations can easily put businesses into real cashflow difficulties and you may find a lender or investor will quickly identify this risk and ask about your contingency plans.

A possible answer to this question may be that you are able to source equivalent products from various parts of the world. This may not be possible if your ability to trade is heavily linked to a specific brand; for example, you have been awarded the exclusive rights to supply a specific brand on the condition that you will not promote or supply any alternatives.

If you have no alternative supply routes you may simply have to build contingency for exchange rate variance into your pricing. Any competitive disadvantage that this entails will have to be off-set; for example with superior service levels or customer convenience.

What's important is that you've considered the issue and understand the impact on your business.

Exit Phase Summary

1. There are different ways of valuing a business, decide which is most appropriate for your business and begin to work towards maximising the valuation.

2. The best valuation and therefore, the best time to plan to exit is likely to be at the top of a growth phase just as you maximise profitability and you're able to show a good history of growth.

3. If you're not intending to exit just as you reach a Stability Step, use the period of stability to add assets to improve your profitability and business valuation.

4. For a business with strong scalability you can overcome the Exit catch-22 by finding an investor who can get you on a steeper growth gradient through specific expertise and contacts rather than simply cash alone.

5. For a business with more limited scalability and less likely to attract an investor, you either need to use an alternative means of finance, or look for a trade purchaser to take a stake in the business earlier. If they already operate in the same market and can bring additional business, this may help you overcome the Exit Catch-22.

6. Consider alternative ways to finance capital requirements or development expenditure to reduce the amount of external funding required.

7. Establish processes and systems to improve your cashflow.

Part Three

Planning for Success

In Part 2 we discussed how the heart of business success can be used to help overcome the various dilemmas and Catch-22s.

We're now going to see how the heart model can be used to structure a business plan.

The process of generating a business plan can really help you to see the way ahead and plan how to get there.

A well-structured business plan is also essential if you need to attract finance from a bank or an investor.

A business plan that is fit for purpose will be easier to implement and monitor progress against; and this will help to ensure you succeed.

Business Planning

Success isn't going to happen by accident, at least not for most of us – you have to plan for it.

A commonly quoted definition is that: 'Success is the completion of anything intended'.

This definition requires you to know in advance what it is that you intend to accomplish. You can think of it as a project and for a project to be successful you need to define it, create a plan and work to that plan to achieve it.

When I first heard the phrase 'if you're failing to plan – you're planning to fail' it was in connection with Project Management and I could immediately see the significance. If you want your project to be delivered on time and on budget to the specified quality, you're certainly going to need a project plan.

But actually, this phrase can be applied very well to running a business. First you need to define the project, which means defining an Ambition Aim with a Time Target. And in order to be sure of success you have to generate a plan showing how you intend to achieve it and that you have the means to achieve it, i.e. the necessary funding.

I prefer the phrase: 'Success comes to those who plan for it'.

In order to plan your route to success, you have to know what level of success you desire for the business and in what timescale.

It's like any journey; you can only plan for it when you know where you are now and where you would like to be.

When I was a small boy I used to be in awe of my Father when we travelled into central London. In a crowded railway station he somehow knew which of the many trains we needed to catch and how it would connect to where we wanted to go.

Of course, now I'm an adult I understand that he knew where he was starting from and where he wanted to arrive, so he was able to plan his travel arrangements and connections.

Just imagine how confusing it would be if you were standing in a crowded station or airport looking at all those travel options but you didn't know where you wanted to go and therefore which option was right for you.

Yet that's exactly what many business owners do with regard to where their business is going. They just start doing rather than planning first.

Your satellite navigation system in your car can only provide you with a route by knowing where you are now and asking you to input a destination.

And there are several routes to choose from; you can ask it to plan the shortest route, the fastest route or the most scenic route.

In business there isn't one single solution because everyone's circumstances and attitude are different; it's whatever is right for you. What speed can you achieve, i.e. what growth gradient can you realistically fund?

When you know what level of success you desire, you will then have to calculate whether your business proposition has the potential to deliver that level of success.

If you have a great idea, but it will cost many thousands of pounds to develop it, you have to be sure that you will be able to acquire sufficient customers to make it worth pursuing.

I see many business owners working very hard, but applying their efforts in a direction that will never produce the reward they hope it will.

Many haven't even made basic calculations to estimate the potential of their venture – they've simply opened for business.

Even a basic outline plan can throw up some useful points that you may not have considered.

The sooner you create a plan the sooner you will know whether you want to pursue it or ditch it.

You will probably need to do some market research or even some market testing, but avoid spending any more than is essential to check the concept and whether it might be sufficiently scalable to provide the kind of returns on your investment that you require.

The more money and effort you've already invested in a venture the harder it will be to walk away from. Even if you know that would be the right thing to do.

There have been many studies investigating why some business succeed whilst most fail and a frequent conclusion is that you're more likely to be successful if you construct a business plan and implement it.

This is partly because the process of creating a business plan means you will need to decide what you're trying to achieve and show that the venture is capable of achieving it.

Your plan will also need to show how you intend to achieve it and what investment is required to fund your chosen route.

Whatever you do, when it comes to business – don't just start doing it.

Let's explore this using the following table showing the four different types of tasks:

Task Types	Process is known	Process is unknown
Goal is defined	2	3
Goal is undefined	1	4

Task Type 1: The process is known but no goal is defined

An example of such a task is when you work on a production line – you know what you have to do each day, but you have no ultimate goal related to that task other than to earn a wage.

People performing such tasks often feel that they have no influence and often feel a lack of job satisfaction.

Task Type 2: The process is known and the goal is defined

As long as you have the skills and tools to perform the task according to the process, you should gain the satisfaction of completing it. An example of such a task is when you collect an item of furniture in a 'flat-pack' for self-assembly.

The instructions are largely pictorial, so as long as you have the required tools and all the pieces are present, you should be able to complete the task to achieve a sense of pride and satisfaction.

There are many such tasks in business and indeed many people only feel comfortable when they're performing this type of task.

Task Type 3: The goal is defined but the process is unknown

In this task type you're given the goal that you have to achieve, but you're left to use your own judgment to decide how best to achieve it.

An example would be that of Sales Director. The sales target for the year and a budget has been defined, but exactly how the budget is spent in order to achieve the target is at the discretion of the Sales Director.

You will only be chosen for the task if the Managing Director believes you have the skills and experience to achieve the task within the budget.

If you achieve it, you will have a great sense of pride and satisfaction and probably a financial bonus as well, because with this type of task your remuneration may be linked to your performance.

Task Type 4: The goal is undefined and the process is unknown

This is the most difficult type of task because nobody tells you what you have to achieve and nobody tells you how to go about it.

Setting up your own business is a 'Type 4' task and perhaps now we can understand why it's so difficult and why the statistics for success are so poor.

In order to be successful at this type of task you need to define where you would like to be in what timescale.

You can then convert your 'Type 4' task into several 'Type 3' tasks, which in turn can be broken down into several 'Type 2' tasks where you have defined the goal and the method; as shown by the arrow in the table below:

Task Types	Process is known	Process is unknown
Goal is defined	2	3
Goal is undefined	1	4

Unfortunately, I meet people who've set up their own business and then just started 'doing' it.

Like all new business owners, they began with a 'Type 4' task, but they haven't recognised it as such. So they haven't defined a goal, a destination or an appropriate level of ambition for the business opportunity.

They've developed a process and gone straight to 'Type 1'; as depicted by the arrow in the table below:

Task Types	Process is known	Process is unknown
Goal is defined	2	3
Goal is undefined	1 ⬅	4

The consequence of going straight to a 'Type 1' task is that you will not only feel a lack of satisfaction, but you are less likely to achieve any real success. Certainly when compared to our second measure of success: what someone else would pay to acquire your business.

This can feel worse than someone working for someone else as described in our original Task Type 1 where they had no control. Because in this case you know that you have the responsibility for control, but you have a sense that you're not exercising that control. This further reduces your level of satisfaction as well as your self-esteem and it's not a good place to be.

This is why, in order to achieve business success, you need to plan for it, rather than just start doing it.

Just a final point on task types; 'life' in general is a 'Type 4' task and this is why when we reach adulthood and no longer have the structure that formal education provides, we can sometimes feel that we've lost our bearings.

Nobody tells us what we have to achieve with our lives. This emphasises the discussion we had in Part 1 about success and significance. What you want to do with your life that's significant can add purpose to your drive for success.

I'm sure you've been asked 'what do you do for a living?' This phrase somehow implies that our work is just a chore that has to be endured in order to be able to live.

Of course many people start their own business precisely because they want a better work/life balance. They want to love their work and be successful.

Unfortunately, I see many people running their own business that have to work so hard that it becomes impossible for them to love it.

I see others who love their work but can't acquire enough customers to make a successful living.

Often with good planning both of these situations can be put right.

Generally, I really enjoy my work, but there's one part that I don't enjoy.

Picture the scene: I'm working with a new client who's spent a good deal of time and money developing their business or business idea or product and is expecting great results.

I've been engaged to help them create a business plan to turn those expectations into reality. We've spent a couple of hours modelling the business on the computer and now we're getting down to the reality of the proposition.

We're looking at the market, the competition, the risks and the scope for success. It may seem hard to believe, but often this is the first time they've really looked at the opportunity properly.

Now they can see exactly how much more cash they would have to invest to make it happen and the extent of the risk balanced against the size of the opportunity.

Their silent contemplation descends heavily in the room.

I know what they're thinking: *"Why didn't I do this at the beginning?"*

And I know what I'm thinking: *"I expect you wish you'd done this at the beginning."*

I'm continually amazed at the lack of planning in small businesses when it's clearly one of the most significant drivers for success.

Yet when it comes to their weekly shop at the supermarket, those same people will have made at least a rough plan to create a list of items to buy. That may mean one plan every week or two for their home life versus none for their business.

What's the worst that could happen if they don't plan their weekly shop? Perhaps they'll suffer a little inconvenience or go without their dessert.

And what's the worst that could happen if they don't plan their business? It goes bust and it's all over.

If they recognise that for a successful shopping trip they need to plan – why would they not recognise that for a successful business they also need to plan?

A common reason people give for not creating a business plan is that there's no point, because it won't turn out like the plan anyway. I'm sure this is really an excuse to avoid all the effort. These are the very people who tend to embark immediately on doing rather than planning first, going straight to Task Type 1.

You've probably seen physical challenges set for teams to achieve – perhaps where they have to cross a river or some obstacle with a limited supply of equipment. The team that wins is always the one that takes time to first consider their solution and plan how to achieve the task before tackling it.

Success requires them to work towards a common goal as a united team. If you're working with partners or fellow shareholding directors, you need to debate and agree the level of ambition and timescale before you can plan how to achieve it.

Consider these 3 drivers for business success:

1. Your proposition – the desirability and value of what you sell

2. Your attitude – a positive attitude outweighs an average proposition

3. Your planning – good planning is not only a significant driver of success in its own right, but impacts the first two as well.

Good planning helps you refine and strengthen your proposition and provides a route to achieving your ambition – this gives you more confidence in your venture, which energises your attitude.

Therefore, you could argue it's the most important of the three.

One of the most significant outcomes of your business plan is the investment required and how you intend to fund it.

Indeed, many business owners seem to think that a business plan is only required in order to raise finance because that's when someone else forces them to produce one.

The bank needs to be satisfied that you're a good risk and that you'll be able to service the debt.

Every investor I've ever met would not invest in a business without first seeing the business plan. They want to judge the return on investment compared with other opportunities.

You may be in the fortunate position of being able to invest in your business yourself, but should you?

You have to create a business plan to check that the venture is capable of delivering to your expectations and to select the options likely to give you the best return on your investment of both time and money.

You can then use the business plan to help you achieve the goals outlined within it.

If you are able to invest in your business with your own cash, I strongly recommend that you treat the investor part of yourself as an alter ego and ask the part of yourself that is the business owner to create a business plan.

I suggest you leave the plan for at least a week and when you read it through again do so as your alter ego – the investor.

Try to be as critical as an independent investor would be. If you put your money in a deposit account you might get a couple of percent return per annum with no risk to your capital. If you invest in a business you would at least want to see more than a couple of percent return because of the higher risk.

Fit for purpose

Like anything, your business plan should be constructed according to its purpose.

The first purpose of your business plan is to show you and your colleagues that the business is a suitable vehicle to achieve your ambition.

The act of constructing a business plan will help you consider your proposition, your market, your growth strategy and the likely return on investment for the funds you employ.

It will help you make your dilemma decisions and work out how you intend to overcome the Catch-22s of growing a business.

A business plan helps to create focus, motivation, confidence and as long as you implement it – success.

For your business plan to continue to be fit for this purpose, it needs to have a structure that enables it to be dynamic; a structure that you can review regularly to keep pace with changing circumstances.

Consider for a moment whether the qualities that make a good traveller would also be good in business.

The philosopher from the 6th century BC and father of Taoism, Lao Tzu (old sage) is credited with saying that *"a good traveller has no fixed plans and is not intent on arriving".*

This would lead us to conclude that the qualities that make a good traveller would not be quite right for succeeding in business.

But actually, it is necessary to have a travel plan; it's just that to get the best from your travels it's good to be flexible. And so it is with a Business Plan.

There are many examples of businesses that have failed because they've held onto their business model after their customers have begun to migrate.

In today's fast moving markets, a Business Plan has to be flexible and dynamic, meaning it should be easy to adapt and quick to amend. So, it should be constructed with flexibility in mind.

The other main purpose for a business plan is to help you raise finance either in the form of a loan in return for interest payments or an investment in return for equity.

If your business plan is aiming to attract a lender it will need to show the risk to their loan capital is as low as possible. This may mean that you will need to show more modest growth so as not to alarm a lender, who will normally have to be conservative in terms of risk.

An investor will compare the opportunity to invest in your business with alternative investment opportunities, so your business plan will need to show the future of the business as optimistically as possible.

Even if you don't require external funding you should still be checking to see whether an alternative approach might enable you or your business to achieve greater ambition or achieve your ambition more quickly.

Business Plan Structure

We can use the heart model to help us define an appropriate structure for a business plan.

As previously discussed, the heart has three critical 'C's, Customers, Capacity and Cash and four links between them:

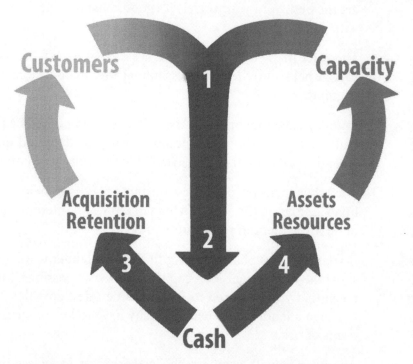

You need cash to fund your strategies for customer acquisition and retention and you need cash to buy assets and fund resources.

But you won't be able to calculate the actual number of customers required and hence the level of capacity you need until you know the extent of your ambition – and this depends on the amount of funding you have available.

The heart needs to be kept in balance as your business grows, so your business plan should show the growing number of customers required to achieve your ambition and the infrastructure required to support those customer numbers.

It will also need to show the cash needed to fund your customer acquisition and retention strategies and fund your assets and resources.

Your business plan can only be developed once you have agreed an Ambition Aim and then the plan can show how you intend to achieve it and the level of funding required.

As we've discussed many times already, your level of ambition must be matched by your ability to fund it.

Therefore, if one of the purposes for your business plan is to get funding, you need to begin the plan with the assumption that you will be successful in obtaining that level of funding.

If you want to avoid rewriting your plan several times, you need to have some knowledge of the level of funding you can reasonably expect to obtain.

The heart model immediately suggests a structure for your business plan with the following headings:

1. Ambition Aim

2. Customers – Acquisition and Retention

3. Capacity – Assets and Resources

4. Cash.

Let's look at each of these sections and see how we will need to expand this structure to make your business plan fully fit for purpose.

Ambition Aim

Remember, the Ambition Aim is only the current level of ambition, so it will relate to what you aim to achieve over the scope of the business plan, typically three to five years.

The level of funding may only relate to the immediate requirement to fund the current Ambition Aim, further funding may be required subsequently.

If your business plan aims to attract an investor you will need to show the current ownership of the business, the level of funding required and the level of equity that may be offered. They will also be keen to know whether there are any existing liabilities in the form of loans.

A potential investor will immediately check the valuation you have currently assigned to the business and whether it seems realistic for the effort you've already exerted. A potential investor will also consider how easily another company could reach the same position.

Potential investors will also want to understand the benefit to them in terms of the likely return-on-investment compared to the risk as well as an indication of their exit options and timescale.

Remember, once a potential investor has put money into your business that money is no longer available for alternative opportunities. So, an investor will want to compare the benefit of investing in your business with the benefit of investing in alternative opportunities.

Information to help an investor make the decision should be shown alongside your ambition so we can expand this section and rename it as the Executive Summary. We'll cover the structure of the Executive Summary in more detail shortly.

The Executive Summary allows the reader to get a good grasp of the whole plan by reading just a couple of pages. A potential lender or investor can then decide whether they're interested enough to read the rest of the document.

Customers

Obviously, your business can only succeed if you offer products and services that customers want to buy in the quantities necessary to meet your ambition.

You will need to provide an analysis of the market with details of your competitors. This will give you and any reader confidence that you can achieve your ambition within the context of the market.

If your ambition would require you to achieve a disproportionate share of the market, you would have to have a highly desirable advantage over the competition that could not easily be copied.

We'll refer to this section in our business plan as:

Market Analysis (Including competitor analysis)

We'll cover this in more detail a little later.

The business plan will need to include details about your customers and how you satisfy their needs with your products and services through convenient channels to earn cash – link 2 of the heart model.

Your Pricing Policy needs to be identified including any quantity buying discounts you intend to offer.

You will also need to identify the impact of your distribution channels on your earnings, for example discounts offered to distributors or commissions paid to agents.

We'll refer to this section in our business plan as:

Products and Services including Distribution and Pricing Policies

Your plan will need to show how you intend to acquire new customers and retain existing customers to achieve your ambition; this is your Marketing Plan – link 3 of the heart model.

The better your customer retention the fewer new customers you need to attain to achieve the same growth gradient, so it is important to also detail any specific customer retention strategies.

We'll refer to this section in our business plan as:

Marketing Plan (Acquisition and Retention)

So, the customer section can be expanded into three sections:

- Market Analysis

- Products and Services

- Marketing Plan.

These sections are covered in more detail later.

Capacity

Your business plan will need to show how your company infrastructure will scale to match your growing customer numbers.

It will show how your business operates and the Assets and Resources you have now and will require as you expand. It can be useful to include an Operational Plan to show why various assets and resources are necessary.

Assets have to be paid for and usually appear on the company's balance sheet; you should include details of key assets both tangible assets, such as property and equipment as well as intangible assets such as trademarks and patents.

Resources require cash but are not owned and will not appear on the balance sheet; the most obvious example is the expertise of your management team and employees.

You should include details of management and employees as well as the systems you have or will need to buy or develop.

One of the reasons you require finance may be to develop systems or buy equipment that will improve efficiency by reducing the capacity required to service the same number of customers. If this is the case, you should show how the profitability will increase and what the timescale would be to pay back the cost of the systems or equipment.

We'll refer to this section in our business plan as: Company Structure

If your business plan is required to attract a lender or investor, they will want to know something about the history of the business or if it's a new business, they will need to know the capabilities and history of the key people to whom they might trust their money.

Although this information can be included within the section Company Structure, it is such an important consideration for a lender or investor that a separate section called Company Background is often included.

This section should explain your present position and how you arrived there.

You will also need to provide details of the background and skills of the key people.

So, the capacity part can be expanded into two sections:

- Company Background
- Company Structure.

These sections are covered in more detail later.

Cash

Your business plan needs to show detailed financial projections, usually over three or five years and would normally include forecasts for the following:

- Profit and Loss (P & L) – income, expenses and profit (or loss)

- Cash Flow – cash movements due to operations, investments and funding as well as taxes

- Balance Sheet – indicates the financial position at a specific time, usually each year-end and includes sources of funds and uses of funds

- Funds Flow – shows how the sources and uses of funds are expected to change over time and the impact on Working Capital.

Lenders and investors will expect to see each financial projection in a recognisable format to enable easy interpretation and comparison with other opportunities.

This section should also identify the maximum cumulative cash requirement, which will need to be funded. If this is to be funded through debt finance, the loan repayments and interest payments will need to be shown in the projections.

These projections are covered in more detail later.

We'll refer to this section in our business plan as: Business Financials.

There is another important consideration that your business plan should address and that is an assessment of the risk and the viability of the business.

Any business opportunity will have an element of risk and you, as well as any lenders or investors, will want to understand and evaluate the extent of that risk.

Your plan will need to include a Business Analysis section where you identify and consider the risks.

This section should include a Sensitivity Analysis, which investigates areas of the business or business plan that will have an impact on the outcome if they are different from your expectations.

The Sensitivity Analysis enables you to demonstrate that you have considered the areas of sensitivity and can explain why you are confident in your projections, for example you may have tested it or done some market research.

Alternatively, you can show how you will implement contingencies that adjust your plan to mitigate for elements that may be outside your control if they occur.

For example, if you cannot acquire customers at the rate you have forecast with the prices you intended, what is the impact on the viability of your business?

The Business Analysis section should also include a summary in the form of the S.W.O.T. analysis, which documents your internal Strengths and Weaknesses and any external Opportunities and Threats.

An example of a weakness may be if you relied on someone with a highly specialised skill essential to your ability to trade. What would you do if that person was absent for several weeks or left permanently?

An example of a threat may be the effect on your business of an increase in the price of an essential raw material, such as oil if you operate a haulage firm or taxi business?

Lenders and investors look at many business plans so they tend to have the insight to quickly identify such weaknesses and threats.

You will soon lose their confidence if they ask you about a potential weakness or threat and you respond as though it's the first time you've considered it.

So, the cash section can be expanded into two sections:

- Business Analysis
- Business Financials.

These sections are covered in more detail later.

Full Business Plan Structure

So, let's see how the full structure for your business plan might look with the additional sections:

1. Executive Summary
2. Market Analysis
3. Products and Services
4. Marketing Plan
5. Company Background
6. Company Structure
7. Business Analysis
8. Business Financials
9. References and Appendices.

The Executive Summary will always come first and References and Appendices will always come last, but you can adjust the order of the rest of the sections to suit the priorities of your particular business and the purpose of the plan.

For example, if you're aiming to start a new business and hope to attract an investor, they will be keen to know the background of the key people before they read your plan in detail. In this case, you may choose to place the section Company Background immediately after the Executive Summary. This shows that you recognise the importance to them of the information in this section.

We'll now take a closer look at each of these sections.

1.Executive Summary

If you don't include an engaging Executive Summary your plan is unlikely to get read at all.

You need to convey the key aspects of the opportunity within a page or two. If a potential lender or investor thinks it will take them any longer to appreciate what's on offer, they won't even bother to start. There are plenty of other business opportunities they can pick up instead.

1.1. Business Statement – what you sell and to whom via which channels and anything that differentiates your business from the competition. If possible, explain the opportunity clearly and briefly within one or two sentences.

1.2. Ambition Aim and Time Target – Explain the scale of the opportunity and ideally, include options for exit, especially if you're aiming to attract an investor with the plan. If the ambition is related to turnover or market share, remember to include a profit aim alongside it.

1.3. Ownership and Target Funds – Who owns the business now, what level of funding is required and if you're giving up equity for funds include the proportion of equity you're offering.

1.4. Customer Summary – An annual summary of the number of new customers, retained customers and market share shown against the turnover projections through the term of the plan. Ideally, this table will also show the marketing spend as a percentage of sales. Experienced lenders and investors will have a good feel for whether you've allowed sufficient funding to achieve the customer numbers required.

1.5. Capacity Summary – An annual summary of the number of employees with sales and profit per employee shown against the turnover and profit projections through the plan. Experienced lenders and investors will have a good feel for the efficiency of utilisation of resources in a particular sector. Investors will be keen to see profit per employee increase as the business grows as this is a good indicator of scalability.

1.6. Financial Summary – An annual summary of the turnover, growth percentage, profit and profit percentage and ideally an estimate of how the business valuation is changing through the life of the plan.

This Executive Summary will give a potential lender or investor greater confidence in you. It shows that you understand your business and that you appreciate the details they may require to make a decision.

For example, they don't have to go hunting through your market analysis to find out how many customers you need to reach your objectives or to scrutinise your Profit and Loss projections to see the level of budget you've identified for marketing to achieve the customer numbers.

The great benefit to you is that your plan will be well received. Even if the reader is not in a position to lend or invest, they are more likely to pass it on to someone else they know who may be more interested in your opportunity.

2. Market Analysis

When you know how many customers and sales revenues you require to achieve your ambition you can check whether this makes sense in terms of the size of the market.

A Market Analysis aims to answer the following questions:

1. What is the customer need that you aim to satisfy with your solution?

2. How many customers have the need and how does this break down to give an annual market size by volume and value?

3. How many competitors are already providing similar solutions?

4. What is the size of the opportunity for you, i.e. potential market share?

5. Is the opportunity sufficient to deliver your Ambition Aim?

Occasionally, something completely new arrives and for a while at least, there appears to be virtually no competitor. There are several difficulties regarding new business concepts:

*   It will take time and money to educate the market about the need for the new product or service. If there are no competitors you have to shoulder the whole burden yourself.

*   There's nobody to learn from, so you have to educate yourself and that usually means some mistakes, which costs money and causes delay. The next entrant, and there will be one if it's profitable, can learn from you and can start from the right place. This can mean that followers may be able to move faster and operate more efficiently. The trail blazer will normally be the market leader at first; the difficulty is hanging on to that position.

- It can be difficult to get anyone to see beyond the risk to fully appreciate the opportunity and agree to lend or invest.

Most businesses even if they're new will have competition where other companies are offering similar products or services to similar types of customers.

Despite the competition, this actually makes it easier to establish a new business because there is is a precedent in terms of knowledge and expectation within the market.

This makes it easier to see how to improve the usual offering and set prices. They will be using their promotional budget to educate the market, for example when new technology means the customer's behaviour needs to change.

The task of analysing the market is more straightforward for an existing concept.

Even though it's easier to conduct a Market Analysis for an existing concept, frequently it's still neglected leading business owners to expect more from their business than was ever likely.

Try the following process to assess your market opportunity, hopefully before you commit too much of your valuable resources.

1. Select a business role model – Consider what you aspire your business to become within the relevant timescale and identify a business that is as close as possible to that image. Ideally it should be operating in the same market and supplying similar products or services. Obtain its turnover figure for the previous year. All companies have to file their accounts and they are usually available online for inspection by the public for a modest fee.

2. The customer – Where is the selected company positioned within the range of customers, for example budget, mid-range or upmarket? If the type of purchase is regular make

an estimate of how frequently they tend to buy. If it's an infrequent purchase, estimate the period before the item is likely to be considered for replacement. This may be because it has passed its useful life, it has been superseded or it is no longer fashionable.

3. The market – Make an estimate of the total number of potential customers in the target customer group within the geographic region of operation. If it's a business-to-consumer market, you might need to look at age and socio-economic grouping. If it's a business-to-business market, you might want to look at the industry sector or the number of employees. Most of this type of data can be accessed via the Internet free of charge or for a modest fee.

4. Products and services – Obtain the price list of the selected company and calculate the average purchase price for a typical customer after usual discounts. Multiply this figure by the number of purchases typically made in a year to obtain the average annual purchase price.

5. Market share – Divide the turnover of the selected business by the average annual purchase price to estimate the number of customers the business may have. Now calculate what percentage this represents of the total market to give an estimate of market share.

Does the market share figure seem reasonable?

You can make this judgement by considering the main competitors to the selected business and whether they are likely to have a greater, equal or lower share of the market.

This is not an exact science, so as long as your figure for market share puts your selected business in about the right position relative to its competitors, it is good enough for our purposes.

If you aspire to become similar to the business you selected, you now have an estimate of your target market share. This is the Ambition Aim, so how long would you like to give yourself to achieve it? Now you can work backwards to fill in the target market share for each of the intervening years.

You might be wondering why I suggested selecting an existing business to assess your target market share rather than simply calculating the market share from your own projections. The reason is simply that it gives a means of checking whether your estimates make sense. If they don't, you can go back over your work and see where you can improve your estimates to more accurately reflect the market.

For you to achieve your target share of the market, there are only two possibilities – either the market is going to grow and you can win a good slice of that growth or the existing businesses will have to move over to let you in.

If there are many competitors in your chosen market, it should be relatively easy to push your way in to join them without them really noticing. Each may take a slight drop in their share to allow you to accumulate yours.

However, if there are only a few competitors, they may well react to a new entrant by adopting aggressive pricing in an attempt to prevent you gaining a foothold. Your Sensitivity Analysis can reflect this by assessing the viability of your business if you can't achieve the target pricing levels. This will inform both your pricing policy and your Sensitivity Analysis.

3. Products and Services

This section should be more than simply a list of your products and services.

It will need to show which products or services are typically bought by which markets or customer types. You will need to show the expected percentage of sales through each channel or from each market.

You can then show the impact on profits due to discounts or commissions applicable for different channels or different markets.

Will you be able to achieve your required sales targets by selling more of your existing products and services to your existing markets? This represents the lowest risk because you're simply expanding what you're already doing.

At some point in your growth, you may need to develop new products or services or sell your products or services to new markets.

This represents an increased level of risk, either because the new products or services are unproven or because your ability to sell to new markets is unproven.

A potential investor will expect to see details of how you intend to grow and how you intend to future-proof your business.

So, you will also need to indicate how you intend to develop your products and services over time to keep pace with the changing needs of your customers.

All of this is only possible if you have sufficient profits or new investment capital to fund new developments. An indication of the expected lifecycle of your products and services and the cost of developing replacements will enable you to calculate your product development budget.

Your business plan will need to show the level of regular expenditure that you have budgeted for research and development.

This section can also show how each product or service contributes to your revenues and profits. This can help you to focus your marketing efforts on attracting more of the customers that purchase your most profitable products or services.

If your customers make regular purchases, you will be able to see how the contributions change over time as you grow the number of retained customers.

This can show the importance of customer retention strategies to ensure you maximise the lifetime value to the business of the customers you acquire. There's more on this in the next section covering the Marketing Plan.

4. Marketing Plan

Marketing covers a wide scope, from market research and discovering the needs of customers to devising the best solutions to meet those needs and then promoting the company and its solutions to win customers.

I use the word 'win' because you're in a race against the competition and the winner gets the prize. You may need to have more than the best products, the best price and being the most convenient – it's about the whole marketing mix and that includes how you communicate with your customers and your potential customers to get your message across.

A company without customers is not a business and I would argue that a plan without marketing is not a business plan. Sales can only result from customers, so I don't like to see sales projections that have no direct link to a marketing plan.

To me, that's just wishful thinking, which is not a very robust route to success.

Some research suggests that a typical customer requires around seven encounters with your brand, from initial awareness through various promotions or promotional material and then direct contact with your company before they're ready to commit to a purchase.

Obviously, this depends on the size and relative risk of the purchase. We're usually happy to hand over some small change for a newspaper to someone standing on a street corner. The larger the purchase and the greater the risk of discovering subsequently that a more appropriate product or solution was available, the longer it takes to make a decision.

If the purchaser is buying on behalf of a company, a significant consideration may be the risk to the purchaser's reputation amongst colleagues.

Developing customer demand takes time, and the more complex the purchase the longer the process is likely to take.

A common concern is whether too much demand could be generated before you have created the capacity to deal with it.

I can understand the concern, because you certainly don't want to upset your customer base and get a poor reputation, but in my experience, it always takes far longer to develop demand than expected. If you find you're too successful, you can always temporarily switch off some of your promotional activities, especially if you're using Internet initiatives and turn them back on when you're ready.

At least you know the likely level of demand you can generate. It's preferable to earning insufficient revenues to cover your capacity.

You need to make a good assessment of the promotional budget you'll need to achieve the numbers of customers required to deliver your ambition. Otherwise, you're in danger of having an unforeseen cash requirement and falling foul of the Growth Catch-22.

As already mentioned Marketing is a big subject, but here we're only going to cover the two elements shown on the heart of business success, Customer Acquisition and Customer Retention. The better your retention the fewer new customers you have to attain to reach the same turnover.

Customer Acquisition

Your promotional activity aims to connect those with a 'need' to your 'solution' to their need. There are a surprising number of promotional options to consider and they won't all be appropriate for your business. Here's a reference list of ideas for consideration in four groups, but with no priority:

1. **Advertising**

    a. Publications – adverts and inserts, directories

    b. Transit media – billboards and buses

    c. Broadcast – television and radio

    d. Internet – search engine, pay-per-click, site referrals, directories

    e. Viral – social spread.

2. **Publicity**

    a. PR – news, editorial, interviews

    b. Sponsorship – choose something or someone with relevance

    c. Competition – make sure you also get some good PR from it.

3. **Promotional Events**

    a. Seminars – great for service-based businesses

    b. Exhibitions – set goals and check the likely return-on-investment

    c. Open days – good for new product launches

    d. Point-of-sale – put a stand at a local event or related site.

4. **Selling**

   a. Networking – good for service-based businesses

   b. Telesales – your database must be current and legal

   c. Direct mail – good if you have an irresistible offer

   d. Direct email – have a call to action, e.g. link directly to a landing page

   e. Direct text SMS – use for existing customers, e.g. your service is due

   f. Referral Marketing – agents, partners, suppliers, customers.

It is also wise to begin with the lowest cost options first and work your way up the scale until you achieve the customer numbers required.

There are many books written about marketing and promotional techniques, so I don't propose to deal with the subject in detail, but planning how you will acquire customers is so fundamental to your success that I feel we must cover a few significant issues.

A 'prospect' is someone who has a current need, is aware that you offer a solution, but has not yet chosen your company in preference to competitors.

A 'Target', which is sometimes referred to as a 'Suspect' is someone who possibly has a need and may not be aware of your solution. You may find that they have just solved their need with a purchase from a competitor and you were too late.

You have two conversion rates to consider:

1. Prospect-to-Customer – an indication of your selling success

2. Target-to-Prospect – an indication of your marketing success.

The aim is to improve both these conversion rates to maximise the return on your marketing spend.

Prospect-to-Customer

Depending on the type of business, you will probably convert prospects to customers by different means or a combination of means e.g.:

- In a prospect meeting
- By telephone
- Via a web site.

Conversion refers to a successful outcome, which is when the prospect says yes and becomes a customer. There may have to be a series of contacts before you succeed.

The conversion rate prospect-to-customer may be quite different for each of these, for example 1 in 3 for a meeting and 1 in 25 for a web site.

Target-to-Prospect

There are many promotional options to generate awareness of your solution to 'Targets'; from personal networking to Internet search engines.

Conversion is when a target makes contact, indicating a current need and becomes a prospect. This conversion rate is likely to be lower than that of prospect-to-customer, for example 5% for networking and 0.5% for Internet search engines. Although you get a higher conversion rate with personal networking, you can only reach a relatively small number of targets.

So the conversion rate has to be considered alongside the volume that you can reasonably expect to target using each method.

If you contact 100 targets and 5 of them make contact, you've achieved a target-to-prospect conversion rate of 5%.

If one of these actually buys and becomes a customer, you've achieved a prospect-to-customer conversion rate of 20%.

The overall conversion rate would be 1%.

You might wonder why you can't simply use this overall conversion rate. But only when you investigate both stages can you clearly see where you need to focus your attention to improve your success.

Consider an Internet Marketing campaign. Suppose you get lots of visitors to your web site, it might mean you're achieving a good target-to-prospect conversion rate. But if few of them ever buy anything, you've got a very poor prospect-to-customer conversion rate. You know that your priority is to make your web site more effective rather than driving more traffic to it.

How many do you need to target?

To create your promotional plan you first need to know how many customers you require to achieve your sales targets.

For example, let's say for a specific month your plan is to acquire 10 new customers. If your conversion rate customer-to-prospect is 25% you will need 40 prospects and if you could achieve a healthy conversion rate target-to-prospect of 5% you will need 800 targets.

It's very easy to say that you want to acquire 10 new customers in a month, but it might be very difficult to network with 800 targets every month.

So you might decide to try direct mail instead.

But the conversion rate will no longer be 5% it may only be 1%, so now you will need to reach 4,000 targets just to achieve 10 new customers.

Alternatively, you could spend some cash on improving your promotional material to enhance your credibility with prospects and as a result you might be able to increase your prospect-to-customer conversion rate to 33%.

To acquire 10 customers you will now need only 30 prospects, which means your direct mail campaign has to reach 3,000 targets. You can save 1,000 letters, flyers envelopes and postage every month. How many months of savings would equate to the cost of the new promotional material?

An additional significant benefit will be that you'll also recoup the time normally taken to meet with 10 prospects. If this is as much as an hour plus an hour of travelling time, you could be recouping twenty hours a month of valuable time.

Or you could use the time to grow more rapidly by acquiring more customers. But don't forget that you'll then have to reach the original number of targets.

Many small businesses underestimate the level of promotional effort required to reach even modest numbers of new customers. That's why they struggle to grow.

Lenders and investors will be experienced in marketing enough to have a reasonable feel for the level of investment required to achieve your stated ambition. They will want to see that the level of spending you've included in your Marketing Plan is appropriate, but they will also want to know how you intend to spend it. They know how easily the marketing budget can be squandered without delivering the sales targets.

Your Marketing Plan should detail exactly how you intend to reach the numbers of targets needed to attract the numbers of customers required to meet your ambition.

Don't forget the likely lag between promotion and the prospect taking action. For a 'big bang' approach, you will need to prepare in advance to minimise any under-utilisation of your capacity.

Successful Promotions

As previously mentioned, it's very easy to waste your limited resources on ineffective promotions. We're so keen to jump at the opportunity for a quick win that we sometimes promote on impulse.

I've done it myself often enough, so I know how hard it can be to resist. I now have a policy never to make impulse decisions when it comes to spending my valuable marketing budget.

The success of any promotional activity is a result of three key elements:

1. Targeting – how appropriate is the message to the person receiving it?

2. Proposition – how well does the proposition compare to the competition?

3. Design – how great is the impact of the message being received?

I have written them in this order because research shows that this is the order of importance with regard to response rate. It doesn't matter how well your design presents your message or how well your proposition compares to the competition if the recipient doesn't have a need or desire for the product or service.

Targeting

Only promote where you're likely to be seen by your target audience. I can't believe how obvious this sounds when it's written down in a simple sentence, but it continues to be a fundamental mistake many businesses continually make.

Imagine the situation where a company has spent hours deliberating over the wording and design of a piece of direct mail. Finally, it's back from the printers and ready to go and they just send it out to the addresses on a database they used a few years ago without bothering to have it checked and cleansed.

I changed the name of one of my companies several years ago and we are still receiving calls from various businesses using the old name, so they are clearly using an old and un-cleansed database.

If your promotion is poorly targeted and you get a disappointing response, it does no good to complain that direct mail is a waste of money.

First, try sending it to a smaller but more targeted audience and see if you get a more reasonable response. If so, you can keep doing it, if not try something else.

Proposition

The proposition refers to the technical performance and design style, the relative convenience and availability, as well as the price relative to equivalent offerings from competitors. If your product is in need of an update it will have to compete on price or convenience, i.e. available immediately from stock.

If you have a strong proposition, you may be able to forecast reasonable response rates.

Any lender or investor will be checking the rates in your plan against their perception of the competitiveness of your proposition.

Design

The purpose of a promotion is to get the message about your proposition across to your target audience and get them to take action.

You need to be sure about who you're communicating with, clear about what message you want to convey and obvious about what action you want them to take.

Let's look at each of these in turn.

Who are you communicating with?

The more you know about and can identify with your target audience, the easier it is to understand their needs and desires and communicate with them in an appropriate style.

This is not always as easy as it sounds because there can be three different people you may need to address for the same sale:

    a. The technical customer – the person who will use the product or service

    b. The financial customer – the person responsible for paying for it

    c. The support customer – anyone who has influence on the buying process.

Here are three examples of this type of relationship:

1. Pupil (a), Parent (b), Teacher (c)

2. Project Owner (a), Building Contractor (b), Architect (c)

3. Production Manager (a), Finance Director (b), IT Manager (c).

In each case the different people are likely to recognise different benefits from the purchase and may respond better to different styles or emphasis in communication.

Therefore, it can be difficult to avoid alienating one whilst at the same time maximising the appeal to another.

A pupil may respond best to the style of promotion that might repel a parent.

The danger is that you end up with something bland and inoffensive to all parties, but not particularly appealing to any.

Even if you don't have identifiable groups like this, it helps to remember that customers are not all the same and can be quite varied.

This is why some companies are trying to find ways of communicating to customers as individuals. They now use technology to change the script depending on the data they hold about people.

What message should you aim to convey?

There's a great deal of material available about how to write marketing messages, but those that tend to work best have two key elements:

1. Differentiation – Explain clearly the benefits of your proposition compared to those of your competitors? What sets you apart?

2. Guarantee – Remove the risk. Provide conviction as to why they should choose your company. Use testimonials, case studies or sales figures, but most importantly, offer some form of guarantee to remove the risk of taking action.

Your differentiation doesn't have to be unique; if it's a good differentiator it will soon be copied. This is why I tend to avoid terminology like Unique Selling Proposition (or Point); is anything really ever unique and if it is, for how long will it remain unique?

Customers are very knowledgeable and with the Internet they have access to the most immediate and comprehensive global information system. They don't like claims that cannot be substantiated or are very unlikely to survive scrutiny. So, I recommend you avoid words like unique, best, fastest or cheapest.

Guarantees can vastly improve your conversion rates, but only guarantee it if you know you can reliably commit to it.

What action do you want them to take?

Ultimately, the objective of your promotion is for the prospective customer to take some action that leads to a sale, so make sure the call to action is really obvious.

It may seem strange that just above I mentioned how wise and knowledgeable people are, yet it's amazing how sometimes we still need to be told precisely what to do. Decide explicitly what it is that you would like the customer to do and then ask them to do it.

Monitor the results

Which promotions work best for your business? If a promotion is worth the effort and cash, it's worth reviewing whether it was successful.

How else will you know whether to do it again?

You've probably heard the old adage: *"I know fifty percent of my advertising works – I just don't know which fifty percent."*

The solution to this problem is referred to as Direct Response Marketing (DRM) where each promotion includes a measurable response from the customer.

Examples of this include:

- Bring this with you to receive your discount or free item

- Mention this code when replying to claim your free item

- Visit this web page to download your free report

- Sign up for our regular bulletin.

Each of these enables you to directly measure the effectiveness of a promotion.

If you're running simultaneous promotions, as you should be, how do you know which promotion actually drove the customer to your door? This is especially difficult if there were several communications that reinforced conviction that your company was the one that deserved the order.

Ideally, you'll include a unique identifying code or response mechanism on each promotion so that you can distinguish between responses.

Internet promotions are usually easier to track because you can use the standard analytics to regularly monitor any referral sites. These are other web pages that have sent traffic to your web site.

Of course, just having the traffic is only part of the process; you need to know whether they took action and ideally whether it turned into business. Web site analytics can also show the route a visitor took through your web site.

Whatever you do it's important that you monitor the results so that you can calculate your return-on-investment. Keep doing the promotions that deliver the best return-on-investment and stop doing the others.

Internet Marketing enables you to quickly test different elements of a promotion; for example, which heading or call to action tends to deliver the best conversion. This can be done using systems that alternate pages to subsequent visitors. You stop using those that work less well and then try changing something else.

Your message or style can become very effective and then continue to remain effective by responding as customers' tastes change.

Low-cost promotions

Employ low-cost customer acquisition options first, as previously mentioned these tend to fall into the following main areas:

1. Viral Marketing

2. Referral Marketing

3. Internet Marketing

4. Public Relations – PR.

These may not all be appropriate for your business and the precise nature of what you do within these broad headings is likely to be affected by the type of business.

I'm not suggesting that all the other options are not required. I'm suggesting that it makes sense to fully utilise the lowest cost options before you begin using those that will consume more cash for similar results.

A combination of methods will work best. This will provide multiple opportunities for prospective customers to get exposure to your brand and your products or services.

Marketing specialists will advise that you need a steady stream of promotions that continually reinforce your message and feed your sales pipeline. Especially if your target audience may need several encounters with your brand before they are ready to buy.

Let's briefly take a look at each of the low-cost options.

Viral Marketing

People love to talk, when they talk about your product or service with no expectation of compensation, that's Viral Marketing. It's called viral because if each person tells a couple of others and each of those tells several others, it multiplies exponentially like a virus.

All you have to do is sow the seeds in a few places and away it goes. Once it's gone you have very little control over the message.

To be effective, you need a memorable and engaging marketing message that people want to transmit to others.

You may wonder what's in it for them. Well, you're exploiting people's natural desire to be sociable and popular. What they get out of passing it on depends on your message, for example:

- If your message offers something of benefit that's free, the person repeating it appears to be doing someone a favour and most of us like to do that. For example, they might just be telling their friends that you're currently running a sale or have a great offer on a particular item until the end of the month or whilst stocks last.

- If your message is current and of-the-moment, the person repeating it appears to be in-the-know and up-to-date. A highly distinctive product will often prompt questions whenever it is used in public. For example, a mobile phone will be seen in both business and social environments and the latest device will often prompt interest – especially from someone currently looking to upgrade their own. Some people even place their new phone on the cafe or boardroom table in front of them as if to really make the point that they're up-to-date. This kind of Viral Marketing has to be built into the design from the outset.

- If your message is entertaining, the person repeating it appears entertaining. My favourite example is the video posted on YouTube by Transport for London titled 'Do the Test' – it begins with a message saying *"This is an awareness test"*. It then shows some youths, half are dressed in black and half in white with a basket ball and you are asked: *"how many passes does the team in white make"*. They begin playing and after thirty seconds or so it stops and gives the answer. It then asks: *"but did you see the moon-walking bear?"* It rewinds and replays the video and this time you see the dark bear moon-walking right across the screen. The message is then delivered *"It's easy to miss something you're not looking for – look out for cyclists."* Apparently, this video was viewed 3.7 million times making it one of the top viral marketing campaigns of 2008.

If Viral Marketing is appropriate for your product or service, it's one of the best low-cost options. The Internet means people can transmit your message instantly right around the world.

Decide what the motivation would be for people to transmit your message to others and then work out how to seed the most influential and socially active members of your target audience.

Referral Marketing

Referrals can come from customers, suppliers, partners or agents. A distinction between viral and referral marketing is one of control.

A message spread virally is not within your control, whereas your referral network can provide feedback and the message can be amended.

This is one of the reasons why I have included Viral Marketing under the promotional category of Advertising and Referral Marketing under Selling. Another distinction is that referral marketing requires regular contact to encourage or incentivise people to continually 'farm' their networks on your behalf.

Your Referral Network is less likely to extend as far from your centre and regular contact enables you to continue to exert more control over the communications.

When you reward them with incentives or commissions you will need a means of tracking who referred the customer to you.

Don't pay commission on order – only pay commission on receipt of payment.

Referral Marketing is your virtual sales team and because you only pay on results, you can grow it as much as you like without having to fund it.

People normally have to have some kind of motivation in order to act and if there is no obvious reward mechanism you have to keep asking and this can be tiresome.

When you have a satisfied customer, make it a habit to ask for a testimonial and who else they know who may have a need for what you do.

You can encourage suppliers to refer people because the more successful your business becomes the more work they will receive from you. It may also encourage you to be more loyal to that supplier.

Consider other businesses that serve the same target market as your business. You may be able to reciprocate with referrals and possibly pay an introducer's commission when you get paid by the customer.

The most likely way that you can extend your virtual sales team is by networking. There are many networking opportunities, so make sure the type of people you would like to meet will be there. Set targets for your networking so you can review how effective the time spent has been.

You may even pick up some business from your networking, but the relatively low numbers means that it will only be worthwhile if customers typically place orders of reasonable value.

It works less well for smaller value sales so use your networking to find partners who can refer business to you.

And as previously discussed, always present an aura of success.

Internet Marketing

The Internet has revolutionised the way small businesses can access their market at low cost. It can put you on a similar level to much larger companies with much bigger budgets.

Some people run very successful businesses from home almost entirely via the Internet.

You have to focus on the customer and the customer's needs. It's no good putting up a web site and expecting the enquiries to come flooding in – because it doesn't work like that.

People search the Internet to satisfy a need and your business will only be successful at using the Internet if your solution to that need can appear on their screen at the point when they action a search.

If you want to attract visitors via the Internet, you will need to be appearing in the listings delivered by Internet Search Engines as a result of key words or phrases being entered.

These are referred to as organic listings to differentiate them from sponsored links which are paid for by the companies appearing in the list.

A placing or ranking of a particular web site on the organic list depends on how well the web site is optimised in relation to the key word or phrase entered by a searcher in a web browser and this is referred to as Search Engine Optimisation (SEO). Essentially, there has to be strong relevance between the search word or phrase entered by a searcher and the information presented on the web page.

There are plenty of free articles within the Internet to help you improve your web site's ranking or you can engage the services of an SEO specialist.

Alternatively, you can pay to quickly get up the search engine rankings using the 'pay-per-click' service offered by the search engines and displayed under the heading Sponsored Links. This means participating in a bidding process and the more you bid per click, the higher you will appear in the rankings. So, although pay-per-click may be quicker, it isn't as low-cost as other techniques that you can employ.

One of the best techniques is to set up what are known as 'landing pages'. Essentially, you provide a one-page web site with a very clear message and usually an irresistible offer. The key is to choose a name for this web page that matches a common search term to drive traffic to it.

Once you've got the prospect to your landing page and they've taken advantage of your irresistible offer, you will usually have their contact details so that you can nurture a relationship with that customer and hopefully get more valuable business from them in the future, perhaps via your main web site.

You can also use other promotional activities to drive traffic to your web pages, both online and off line. An integrated approach usually delivers the best results.

Getting prospects to your web site is only the first part of the process – you have to entice them to take action.

Public Relations – PR

PR can reach relatively large audiences at low cost if you can get editorial coverage without having to purchase advertising space alongside your editorial. For the amateur, this can take time and a little practice, so you may have to engage the services of a PR consultant and this will increase the cost. It may still be low-cost and represent a good return-on-investment.

First, you need to decide on the publication, whether you will aim for local coverage in the local free newspapers or wider coverage in a national paper or magazine.

Research which publication your target market is likely to read.

Once you know that, you can start reading the publication regularly to understand the style and find out the process and deadlines for contributions.

If your item relates to a particular time of the year, you may have to submit your press release three to six months in advance. If your item is in response to a current news event, you will have to move very fast to not miss the wave of interest.

Another issue with PR is that it can create a sudden surge of interest, which quickly dissipates. You have to be ready for this surge, so if you sell from stock make sure you have some before you release your PR.

You can do more damage to your brand through poor PR or poor response to that PR than by not doing any in the first place.

The secret to good PR is to understand the motivation of the people that have to fill their space with good quality copy by the deadline. So, if you can provide them with what they need, you're more likely to get published.

Again, the more confidently you present your article, the more likely you are to get published.

Successful low-cost promoting

Successful low-cost promoting requires your brand name to be memorable.

We don't tend to remember phone numbers or complicated web addresses.

Internet Marketing can send messages around the web with click through links, but if you want to create a buzz outside of the Internet, you can't rely on people taking a pile of your literature with them where ever they go.

Your brand name has to be transmitted by word-of-mouth, which means it has to trip off the tongue easily and register in the brain of the recipient.

Then, when they go to look it up, usually on the Internet, the search engine needs to be able to point them to your web site, which will also provide your other contact details.

I sometimes hear people say that small businesses shouldn't worry about trying to build a brand. I hope what they mean is that you shouldn't spend your valuable marketing budget on promotions that are purported to build brand awareness rather than achieve sales. In this case I agree and I would also suggest that large companies shouldn't run promotional campaigns that don't aim to deliver sales.

But even a small company needs to have a memorable brand name and a means by which customers can contact you by knowing your brand name alone.

I remember a new independent cafe opening near where I live and it had a good location with plenty of visibility. It was well presented and seemed to offer everything it needed to be a success. But it had one major failing that I noticed immediately – I remember pointing it out to my wife and commenting that it wouldn't last long – and it didn't.

The name of the cafe was in stylised writing that was hard to read. This made it much more difficult for people to suggest it as a place to meet for coffee. Look at all the successful cafes and you'll see how easy they are to read, remember and transmit.

To make best use of most low-cost promotions, you need to check the following:

- Can you verbally impart your brand name to a stranger and can that person reliably remember it?

- If a person only knows your brand name can they enter it into an Internet search engine and find your company web site and contact details?

To achieve the first of the above you need to avoid strange spellings that may work well on paper, but just get in the way when spoken. You should also avoid long names unless the name is some kind of easily transmitted sentence.

If a search engine does not show your web site listed on page 1 of the results when your brand name is entered, you need to embark on some Search Engine Optimisation (SEO). A good place to begin is to ask your web site designer, because this really should have been part of the original brief.

Customer Retention

The heart of business success shows cash flowing out to acquire customers.

The better your customer retention the lower your customer acquisition rate needs to be to achieve your growth gradient.

Alternatively, with a better customer retention rate you can grow faster for the same customer acquisition rate.

There may be additional benefits as well. For example, when you can explain clearly to a prospective customer how you keep your existing customers satisfied, it is likely to improve your prospect-to-customer conversion rate.

This might reduce the amount of capacity deployed in the process of prospecting customers or for the same amount of time, increase the number of prospects you can see.

Even if you don't have to 'see' prospects, it is likely to reduce your cost-of-acquisition.

Whatever your cost-of-acquisition, you can improve your profits when you don't have to acquire so many customers to achieve your sales target because you're retaining them for longer.

So, it really should be a priority to keep existing customers satisfied and retain them for as long as possible.

Yet it seems to be one of the most neglected areas of business. Existing clients are continually taken for granted in the pursuit of new customers, for example:

- Offers are only available to new customers

- A customer with a problem is treated as a nuisance rather than an opportunity.

By contrast, if you switch your focus to the *Lifetime Value* of a customer, it can dramatically improve your profitability.

You can aim to improve the *Lifetime Customer Value* by increasing the scope of what you sell and lengthening the time over which you retain them as a customer.

To estimate the typical *Lifetime Customer Value* first estimate the average order value and the frequency that customers tend to order. Now consider the length of time a customer may typically remain with the company. You can then calculate how many repeat orders are likely within the typical customer retention period and multiply it by the average order value. This will be the average amount of revenue earned over the typical customer lifetime.

The *Lifetime Customer Value* can then be estimated by subtracting the average cost of acquisition and any costs you can directly attribute to servicing and retaining them.

Now decide how long you would like to try to extend the time a customer remains with the company. Remember that you won't be able to control every reason why a customer may leave, but you can have an impact on customer satisfaction.

Suppose you target an increase in the typical customer retention period of 25%. You can estimate how much additional revenue you will earn and subtract the cost of servicing them. But you don't need to subtract the cost of acquisition this time.

I then recommend using the rule of thirds so you can take a third of the additional profit you will earn as the budget to fund the customer retention policies that you will introduce to achieve the 25% increase in retention period and leave two thirds to flow through as extra profit.

You now have a specific budget for implementing your customer retention policies. Of course, you'll have to fund this budget initially until the results feed through to your bottom line and it becomes self-sustaining.

There are various different policies you can employ to improve customer retention depending on the type of business. I don't have the space to deal with such a large subject here, but there are plenty of other books you can read on the subject.

Generally, they all aim to extend retention by improving customer satisfaction.

The key to improving customer satisfaction is to meet or preferably exceed their expectations.

Suppose you buy a bottle of perfume from a respected Department Store and when you get it home you find the packaging is damaged. Even though the main item inside is perfectly alright and you're only going to discard the packaging, you're still left with a negative impression of the retailer because your experience didn't match your expectations.

However, if you had purchased exactly the same item complete with the same damaged packaging, but this time from a discount retailer, you may be left with no negative impression because your experience and your expectations were still reasonably aligned.

There is now over-supply in virtually every market, which usually means there are many options from which customers can select. Your company's satisfaction levels have to be class-leading to maximise customer retention.

You would imagine that small companies have the edge over larger rivals when it comes to customer satisfaction and loyalty, but they frequently have insufficient capacity to deal with surges of demand.

As soon as customers experience a problem, they begin to question their loyalty. The way your company responds to a problem is critical to maintaining customer loyalty.

This means that there are two areas to focus on:

1. Prevent problems from occurring in the first place

2. Respond to problems in a way that maintains customer satisfaction.

Suppose a customer requests delivery of an item on Monday, but you explain that you can only get it to them on Tuesday. They might be disappointed, but they are not dissatisfied. You have managed their expectation and hopefully, retained them as a customer.

Whereas, if you allow them to believe it will be delivered on Monday and it isn't delivered until Tuesday, they will be both disappointed and dissatisfied.

Suppose that you really expected it to be delivered on Monday and so you told the customer to expect it on Monday, but then a problem occurred that meant it now couldn't be delivered until Tuesday.

The business with a focus on customer satisfaction will take the trouble to telephone the customer and apologise for the delay and so mitigate for some of the dissatisfaction.

Whereas, a business that doesn't make that call is sending a message that it doesn't care, which leads customers to perceive that their business isn't valued by the company; so they are more likely to take their business elsewhere.

Customer satisfaction is often about creating a company ethos of valuing a customer and that has to start at the top – with the owner of the business.

If you give the impression that a customer with a problem is a nuisance, your employees will take their lead from you and your retention period will suffer.

However, if you treat a customer with a problem as an opportunity to show that customer how much you value their business – they can become more loyal than if they had never had the problem in the first place.

This is because you have proved to the customer by your actions that they are valued. Despite having experienced a problem they remain loyal because they don't know that an alternative supplier would have performed so well in similar circumstances.

Customers are realistic enough to know that problems will occur, so first make sure problems aren't likely to occur through negligence and then if a problem does occur make sure your employees feel empowered to rectify it expediently.

Aim to embed processes within your systems that flag up potential problems, if possible in advance and otherwise as soon as possible afterwards. Then aim to rectify the problem and contact the customer before they have to contact you.

Communication is a key component of customer satisfaction, which can extend the average customer retention period and improve profitability.

I remember working on customer retention for a client and needed to understand why some customers hadn't ordered for a while. I took names of about twenty customers who hadn't ordered lately and called them.

I introduced myself as being independent, and that I had been engaged by my client to evaluate customer service. Not only was the information invaluable in developing policies, but also within a couple of days, several of them contacted the company saying how impressed they were that a business was interested enough to call them. Some even placed orders for the first time in years.

If a customer does stop ordering, it can be really useful to find out why. Even if it's for a reason that you can't change, the fact that you showed that you cared may lead them to recommend you to someone else who does have a current need.

If your business attracts regular repeat orders from retained customers, it is worth including in the Marketing Plan a section on Customer Retention with an estimate of Lifetime Customer Value for different types of customers.

You might also show how you expect this to change over the timescale of the plan - for example:

- You intend to launch additional products or services to increase sales values

- You intend to introduce systems to manage the customer relationship better and extend the retention period

Customer retention is an important consideration to maximise Lifetime Customer Value and minimise the level of marketing spend you need to include in your plan to achieve the same growth gradient.

5. Business Background

Prospective lenders or investors will look at where you are now and consider whether they believe it to be a viable platform to begin the journey described in your business plan.. They may really like the opportunity, but consider that you're not yet in the right place to go for it.

Have you heard about the couple driving through the countryside and realise that they're completely lost. Perhaps, their satellite navigation system was faulty. They see a man by the side of the road and stop to ask directions. He considers their predicament for a moment before replying: *"Well, if you want to go there – I wouldn't have started from here".*

I like this tale, because it's so simple and yet contains a clear message – the best or most direct route is not always possible.

I don't know if you know much about sailing, but you'll know that a sailing boat uses the power of the wind and therefore, if you want to go in the direction the wind is blowing from, you can't go directly there because you can't push against the wind.

So, you have to perform a zigzag route. You sail as close to the wind as you can on a 'zig' leg, then tack and sail as close to the wind as you can on the 'zag' leg.

Eventually, you can get where you want to go, but you have to persevere with the frustration of an indirect route.

In the Introduction of this book I mentioned that a familiar example of a Catch-22 occurs in the context of job searching – to apply for a job you require relevant work experience, yet to obtain the necessary work experience you need a relevant job.

The way to overcome this Catch-22 is not to expect to go straight there, but to zigzag. A change of career can be either a change in job function or a change of the field in which you work.

Take a look at the change of career table below:

B New job function Current field	D New job function New field
A Current job function Current field	C Current job function New field

Change of career table

It may be unrealistic to expect to be able to change your job function and your field of experience in a single leap, i.e. going from quadrant A directly to quadrant D.

It is more viable to first attempt a change of job function in your current field, quadrant B or a change of field with your current job function, quadrant C.

The same is likely to be true with your business. The market in which you trade is equivalent to the field in our career table and the products or services you intend to offer would be equivalent to the job function.

Consider whether the route to your ambition can be direct because you're planning to do more of the same; or whether you're attempting to diversify by developing new products as well as selling to new markets.

You may have to make more of a zigzag route to reduce the risk. Develop new products in a market you're familiar with or move into new markets with products you're familiar with. Changing both at the same time represents the highest risk.

When we first discussed the link between Customers and Capacity in the heart model, link 1, we considered how success is more likely if you have the necessary expertise, equipment and capacity to provide a particular solution.

Lenders and investors will want to know whether the management team has the necessary skills and experience to succeed in your stated ambition and your past achievements will be taken into consideration.

The better your track record in the specific market or with the types of products or services you intend to offer, the more likely you are to be successful in obtaining finance.

If you think potential lenders or investors may have concerns, you can add some supporting text in this section to explain why you believe you will be successful.

You can include details of any employees outside the management team with expertise that is crucial to the company's ability to succeed.

It helps you to ensure that you've included any relevant details, but try not to pad it out with long life histories of people. One or two carefully scripted paragraphs should be enough for most of your key people.

Some people don't like to talk about themselves and feel awkward about compiling this section, especially when the business plan is only for internal use.

However, I believe it can fulfil two important purposes:

1. It gives you conviction that your team has the necessary skills and experience to succeed with the venture

2. It can highlight any areas where the team needs to be strengthened.

You will find that a potential investor will be evaluating this section with these two points in mind. Sometimes a condition of investment is that you strengthen the management team with a particular expertise and they may even nominate someone to work on a part-time basis.

Of course, the salary for any additional people will have to come from the business, which may affect the amount of funding required.

6. Company Structure

This section would normally include details of the way your business operates. Some larger businesses actually employ an Operations Director. Responsibilities of the Director of Operations will typically include manufacturing and logistics.

Even smaller businesses can benefit from identifying the work flows or processes in an Operational Plan for the business:

- An Operational Plan can help ensure you've included all the assets and resources you might need. This is especially important if the business hasn't already been operating the necessary processes; for example if it's a new venture for the business.

- An Operational Plan can also help you justify why particular assets or resources are necessary. It can be difficult to justify an asset or resource if it can't be linked to an essential part of the operational process, i.e. winning it, doing it or getting paid for it.

If the business is already quite large or is expected to grow rapidly, the Company Structure section should include an Organisation Chart showing management, divisions, outlets or departments.

But be careful not to overdo it.

A potential investor will get nervous if you present a complex organisation structure that will devour cash at a rapid rate.

We discussed previously the importance of keeping control of the costs associated with capacity until appropriate. You don't want to find that you're having trouble funding customer acquisition activities because it's all been spent on building your infrastructure.

Complex organisation structures also tend to complicate communications, reduce efficiency and can stifle creativity.

Beware of the so called 'silo' mentality. A silo is a building used for storage that usually has no windows. The term has been used to describe companies where parts of the organisation seem to work in isolation from each other.

Modern companies tend to operate with more flexible structures and relatively few tiers of management. They prefer to empower employees to make decisions without management intervention and use systems to keep control.

The benefits of a flexible structure are that it tends to improve customer service and costs less. It can also react more quickly because decisions are taken as close as possible to the point of impact, which is usually where the knowledge of the issue is most detailed. This means it can identify opportunities for improved efficiency and enhance creativity.

Empowered employees tend to feel more engaged with the business and are more productive.

Although this type of structure has many benefits, it is sometimes resisted by management because it can feel like they have less control, especially if they are used to a more traditional structure.

Introducing systems will provide control and enable management to manage-by-exception. This means that they only need to intervene when a decision falls beyond the levels delegated to the person normally responsible.

This is another example of how systems can enable management to work 'on' the business rather than 'in' the business.

The Company Structure section will also provide details of the the Assets and Resources that you already have and that you will require as your business expands.

If new equipment or systems will improve efficiency, you can indicate how you will be able to reduce the company infrastructure as a result. Don't forget that if you're buying equipment, Asset Finance may be the most appropriate funding option.

7. Business Analysis

This section may include a Sensitivity Analysis and a S.W.O.T. Analysis.

Sensitivity Analysis

There are usually several key parameters that determine the viability of the business and the aim of this analysis is to see how sensitive your projections are to these parameters.

You can assess the risk and hence viability of your business plan by reviewing the projections when these key parameters are set to worst case, target case and best case.

If it remains viable with all key parameters set to worst case, you can proceed with maximum confidence and the business plan can be classified as Low Risk.

However, it is more likely that the Sensitivity Analysis will suggest levels of viability as shown in the following table:

Sensitivity Analysis	Worst Case	Target Case	Best Case
Highly Viable			√
Viable		√	
Not Viable	√		

In the above example we can see that if every key parameter hit worst case the business would not even be viable.

If Debt Finance has been used to cover the cash requirement the lender would prefer to see that you can still service the debt repayments and interest payments even if each key parameter hits worst case. Clearly this is not the case in our example above and because the interest model makes lenders very risk averse they may decline.

An investor will have more flexibility and will weigh the risk against the potential reward. In this case it is necessary to make considered judgements about the likelihood that every key parameter would hit worst case. It is much more likely that some will be below target, some will be on target and some may even be better than target.

You will need to consider what mitigating and contingent actions can be included within the plan to improve all your worst case predictions.

The more process and systems you can implement to improve the worst case position in advance, the more you can reduce the level of risk.

Sometimes, this can be achieved by identifying a parameter as key to the viability of your plan and regularly monitoring it.

If the parameter is largely within the control of the business, the regular attention may be sufficient to prevent it ever reaching worst case.

Below is a short list of some examples of possible parameters to consider for your business. You will need to assign figures for worst case, target case and best case for each parameter and check the impact on the viability of your business:

1. Average Selling Price

2. Average Costs, especially key costs such as oil

3. Average Sales Value

4. Occupancy Rates

5. Customer Purchase Frequency

6. Conversion Rates: Prospect-to-customer and target-to-prospect

7. Customer Payment Period

8. Customer Retention Rate

9. Overheads, especially Salary rates or rent rises.

The specific type of business is likely to affect what is most critical and some of which maybe outside your control, for example:

- Retail sector – a key parameter maybe 'footfall', i.e. the number of people passing along the street, which may depend on the weather or the general economic climate.

- Holiday sector – key parameters maybe the weather or the exchange rate.

- Haulage – a key parameter maybe the price of fuel.

If a key parameter for business viability isn't within the control of the business, you need to devise contingent actions to ensure viability if the parameter moves outside its target range.

This type of Sensitivity Analysis will show that you've considered the risks and how you can mitigate for each of them. This is great for your own confidence and can really help you obtain finance.

S.W.O.T. Analysis

The Strengths and Weaknesses are generally internal to the organisation and the Opportunities and Threats are generally external to the organisation.

It's important to have defined a specific objective before you conduct your S.W.O.T. analysis because an identified strength for one objective might be a weakness for another.

The aim of the S.W.O.T. analysis within the scope of a business plan will show how you intend to:

- Capitalise on each strength

- Improve each weakness

- Exploit each opportunity

- Mitigate for each threat.

Most lenders or investors will expect to see this kind of analysis within a business plan.

Some people are nervous about highlighting their weaknesses or threats to a potential lender or investor. Obviously, you don't want to highlight something that will significantly weaken your case. However, if they are likely to recognise a weakness or threat anyway, it is preferable to show that you've already identified it and considered how to mitigate any negative impact.

For example, if your management team is weak on marketing or finance, you can identify it within the Company Structure section and explain that you will recruit expertise as soon as you get the funding and that you've included the salary in your projections.

There are two types of actions you can highlight in your business plan:

1. Preventative – actions taken to remove the cause of a potential problem or minimise the probability of it arising

2. Contingent – actions taken to minimise the effect of a problem once it has arisen.

If the problem is within your control, preventative actions typically cost less than contingent actions.

Let's take a look at the example of the sudden absence of a member of the team with a specific skill that's critical to earning revenues. A preventative action may be to train or recruit additional capacity, or begin outsourcing the function. A contingent action might be to outsource the service only when absence occurs

Lenders will be particularly keen to see that you've considered the threats and have strategies for dealing with them so they can have confidence that you will still be able to service the debt even if the threat occurs.

Investors will be particularly interested to see any opportunities that might extend the scope of the return on their investment. You will want to present the opportunities to encourage an investor to select your business in preference to alternative business plans they may also be reviewing.

If you have only one or two key competitors a good way to show how you will be able to gain a competitive advantage is to conduct a brief S.W.O.T. analysis for each of them as well. You can then draw comparisons between them and your own or show how your strengths exploit their weaknesses.

If you choose to include a competitor's S.W.O.T. analysis in this section it would be worth making reference to it in the Market Analysis section. Alternatively, you could include it as an appendix and refer to it here and in the Market Analysis section.

8. Business Financials

The Executive Summary will already have given summary figures from the business financials, but an interested lender or investor will also want to see full financial projections within your plan. The Business Financials section should include projections for at least three years for profit and loss, cash flow, balance sheet and funds flow.

The Profit and Loss forecasts how much the business expects to earn each month from selling its products and services and the cost of those sales to provide a gross profit. It then shows the expenditure on overheads each month to forecast a net operating profit.

The Cash Flow forecasts the flow of cash in and out of the business each month. The cash flow has to take account of any delay between invoices sent to customers and receipt of payment as well as any delay between the company receiving supplier invoices and issuing payment.

However, Cash Flow projections are not simply time-shifted Profit and Loss projections. There are some significant differences between them, for example:

- Value Added Tax (VAT) is collected on sales on behalf of the Government or paid on expenses and will appear in the cashflow, but not in the Profit and Loss. The cash flow will show the additional receipts and payments due to VAT each month and then when due - usually each quarter. show the net VAT payment to the Government.

- Loan receipts and repayments are included in the cashflow, but only interest payments are shown as an expense in the Profit and Loss.

- Capital Expenditure used to purchase assets is included in the cashflow, whereas depreciation of assets is shown in the Profit and Loss.

You need to familiarise yourself with your financials so that you can answer any questions. It's very easy to run them off or receive them from whoever has compiled them and not inspect them properly.

Take the time to review your projections and consider what the reader of your plan might want to ask and ideally have supporting data to hand.

A lender will want to check that your projections take into account any seasonal effects. Even businesses that don't have specific seasonality will tend to see reduced activity during peak holiday periods. These periods may see a reduction in the level of invoicing, but not a reduction in costs because rents and salaries still need to be paid.

If your cash flow appears tight, a lender may want to check the implications of such seasonality. For example, if the reduced level of invoicing in December translates to a reduction in cash receipts some weeks later, could it coincide with the net VAT payment being due to the Government?

If a lender realises you could have a cash flow problem and you haven't recognised it, they may become concerned about your ability to manage your cash flow.

They may also ask you about the break-even point. As the term suggests, this is the point at which costs and profits are equal, so there is no net loss or gain.

A lender may be interested to look at your break-even because they want to see the level of sales required to cover your costs. They will assess how realistic this seems when considering the risk of lending to your business.

You may want to explore how feasible it would be to reduce the level of sales required to break-even by improving your gross margin, either by increasing your prices or by negotiating better costs. You should also look at opportunities to reduce overheads and improve your net margin.

Whilst it can be useful to know how much gross margin is required to break-even each month, I'm concerned about placing too much emphasis on it.

I've mentioned earlier that you're more likely to hit what you aim at, so if you focus on break-even, you can guess what will happen – you'll break-even and that means zero profit, no reinvestment and the slippery slope to decline.

We've discussed some of the aspects that a lender may look at, let's think about it from an investor's perspective. An investor will want to see steady growth on the sales line and then check whether the net profit percent of sales is increasing to indicate the potential scalability of the opportunity.

It may not be showing an increase because you've taken the additional profit and ploughed it back into the business, for example by adding assets and resources.

If this is the case, you could write a quick note to that effect so the investor can be guided to a better conclusion than a cursory glance at the figures may suggest.

The Balance Sheet is a snapshot of the business at a point in time. Many business owners have real problems getting to grips with it. Essentially, it is making sure that at a specific point in time the source of funds and the use of funds equate:

- The use of funds:

  □ Fixed assets – buildings, vehicles, equipment

  □ Current Assets – cash reserves, stock, debtors.

- The source of funds:

  □ Liabilities – creditors, e.g. suppliers not yet paid, Director's Current Account (usually bills settled on behalf of the business by a Director or deferred salary owed to a Director)

  □ Loans – including Director's Loan Account

  □ Shareholder's funds – capital provided by shareholders, retained profit.

A balance sheet does not show how profitable a business is or show the true market value of its assets. It shows the Net Book Value of assets, which is the purchase costs less the depreciation to date, but this is not necessarily the amount that could be recouped if the assets were sold at that time.

The Balance Sheet can be an important document for a potential investor. For example, the Balance Sheet may indicate that you or other Directors or shareholders have provided cash to the business and built up a significant liability for the business. Effectively, the business owes the directors and/or shareholders this money, usually referred to as the Directors Current Account for items outstanding for a shorter time and the Directors Loan Account for longer-term lending.

A condition frequently imposed by a potential investor is that the liability represented by these Director's Accounts is either written off or converted to shares. This is because a new investor will want the cash they are about to invest to be used to develop the business rather than to pay off existing liabilities.

The Funds Flow Statement details the sources and uses of funds and will indicate the change in Working Capital over a period as well as the reasons for that change.

Working Capital is defined as Current Assets less Current Liabilities. Working Capital is a measure of how easily a business can fund its operations and service its debts as they fall due. If Current Assets are less than Current Liabilities the business is said to have a Working Capital Deficit.

If the Funds Flow Statement shows Working Capital to be increasing, the business has either increased its Current Assets or decreased its Current Liabilities.

A business can be profitable and have assets, but still lack liquidity if its assets would not easily convert into cash.

The term over-trading applies when a business grows too quickly for its liquidity and becomes unable to pay its bills or service its loans as they fall due.

We can see how easily this can happen by considering the movement over a period within Current Assets. Funds could move from cash reserves into stock and then be traded so they now appear in debtors. The total figure for funds within Current Assets could be the same, but the level of liquidity has changed.

When the funds were in the form of cash reserves, they were highly liquid. When the funds were in stock they were far less liquid because a buyer would need to be found before stock can convert back into cash. Suppose the business was so keen to grow that it chose to ignore its normal credit checking procedures for its customers – some of the funds may now be in debtors that take longer to collect or may never convert back into cash.

Over-trading is a common cause of businesses requiring quick access to additional funding. If it can't obtain the required funding, the business may be forced to urgently liquidate assets at a loss or cease trading.

A lender or investor may want to look at the trend in the flow of funds before agreeing to invest.

You can see how important it is to be aware of what potential lenders or investors are looking for in the figures and for you to be familiar with those figures. Then you can think about your response in advance and confidently answer any questions.

There is more on this in the section on pitching to an investor.

References and Appendices

If you refer to published statistics or research within your plan you should detail references to show credibility and indicate that you're happy for them to be verified.

Use appendices for supporting information that you need to provide to reinforce your position. Before you include anything extra, always make sure you can answer questions on it. Leave it out if there is any possibility that its inclusion could embarass you or be detrimental to your case. If in doubt - leave it out.

Implementing your Business Plan

Compiling a business plan can be extremely beneficial, but the benefits will be multiplied if the plan is actually implemented and progress against it is monitored.

You've put a great deal of effort into thinking about and creating your business plan, so please don't shove it in a drawer and forget about it.

This is a frequent occurrence when a business owner created a plan primarily to raise finance. If the plan was successful in raising finance, it probably means the lender or investor recognised that if the plan was implemented the business would succeed and they would benefit.

I like to make the distinction between creating a business plan and then implementing it as similar to the concept of working 'on' your business rather than 'in' your business.

Just as there is no point working 'in' your business if you never give any thought to where it is going or what you're trying to achieve – there is no point thinking about where your business is going if you never do anything about getting it there.

Developing your business plan and then regularly reviewing the opportunities for modifying it to make it even more effective are times when you are working 'on' your business.

Implementation of the business plan has two stages, the first stage is creative and the second is operational.

The creative part is also working 'on' your business and that is to amend your processes and systems to reflect your business plan and any amendments to it.

Operating the processes and systems is working 'in' your business, but this can now be handed over to others.

Only when your processes and systems for implementation are fully aligned with your ambition, timescale and funding will you achieve success.

The operational stage should be delegated as much as possible because this is the daily process of running your business according to the processes and systems that you have established.

We'll come back to this in a moment, but first I want to revisit the common reason people give for not creating a business plan – that there's no point, because it won't turn out like the plan anyway.

Implementation is critical to making it happen the way you want it to happen.

We have to remember that we're predicting the future, which is always uncertain.

The only thing we know for certain is that the forecasts in a business plan will always turn out to be wrong. Hopefully, you'll exceed your forecasts, although the reality is that most plans turn out to be optimistic.

Yet even that doesn't matter.

I remember working with a new client who was absolutely unable to define an Ambition Aim, even just for the coming year. I tried everything to cajole him into making some kind of goal, so that at least he had ownership of it.

In the end I had to suggest an Ambition Aim for him and then ask him if he would be prepared to strive for it. He agreed and on that basis we were able to create a business plan.

The very next day he telephoned me to say how wonderful he felt about having this goal and that although he felt it was a stretch, he thought it was achievable.

It transpired that he didn't actually achieve it, but he got much closer than he would have imagined possible before we set it.

And here's the real point to the story, let's suppose he didn't set the target and just carried on doing. Let's suppose that he arrived at the end of the year having achieved half the figure we actually chose to set as a target.

How might he have felt? I expect he would have simply felt ambivalent, neither pleased nor displeased. Yet, having achieved much more by working towards a target, how did he actually feel? Well, he was pleased and at the same time slightly disappointed.

Sometimes when I'm speaking to business groups I use the following script, which is based on one of my own goal-setting experiences:

"My target for this month was 100k. It looks like I've hit about 80k. Am I disappointed? – A little; am I happy? – Of course, because I know that if I hadn't aimed for 100k, I'm more likely to have hit only half what I achieved and ended up with 40k. And that's because you're more likely to hit what you aim at. Once you know what you're aiming at, you can develop strategies to hit it.

Judging by the way you're all looking incredulously at me, I can only assume that you think my 100k this month refers to money – but unfortunately no, it refers to 100 kilometres of running. I was aiming to complete my usual 10km run 10 times in the month, but only managed 8. That's twice a week, but if I hadn't aimed for the big 100k, I probably would have settled for 1 run a week and that's only 40k. If I had been talking about money – the principle is exactly the same: you're more likely to hit what you aim at."

The best way to achieve something large is to break it into smaller, more manageable, chunks.

At the beginning of this part of the book we discussed the different types of task and creating your business plan was the first step in achieving your Type 4 task because you've now defined your ambition.

So, now you know what you're trying to achieve, it's no longer a Type 4 task, but has become a Type 3 Task or several Type 3 Tasks.

However, Type 3 Tasks can't be implemented because they have a target but no process. So we have to break each Type 3 Task into one or more Type 2 Tasks, where the process is also defined and therefore can be implemented.

The interim stage that I mentioned earlier between creation of your business plan and its implementation is where you break it into more manageable chunks, each of which has a target and a defined process. You should also systemise each process to ensure reliability and consistency.

Break up your targets into annual, quarterly, monthly, weekly or even daily targets so that you and everyone else in the business can focus on regular progress and celebrate your success.

Let's look at how this might work in practice by considering two parts of the typical business process:

1. Winning customers

2. Increasing the average order value.

Winning customers

In the marketing section of the plan we discussed how the number of new customers you require in order to achieve your sales targets will depend on the average order value.

Once you know how many customers you need each month you can use your prospect-to-customer conversion rate to calculate how many prospects you need and then use your promotional target-to-prospect conversion rate to work out how many promotional targets or suspects you need to reach that many prospects.

Implementation means making sure your business is hitting the required levels of promotional activity each month. You know the target, now you need to make it happen and monitor it to make sure that it continues to happen.

You may have somebody responsible for this or you may choose to out-source it to a marketing agency.

Your role will still be to monitor progress against your targets and implement any corrective action if you fall short of target.

Increasing the average order value

Once you have customers, you can create processes to maximise the value of those customers, perhaps using cross-selling and linked-selling:

- Cross-selling – This is the process of ensuring that customers are aware of the benefits of other products or services in your range. The customer may benefit through greater convenience and having fewer transactions. Process can make it automatic so that the right questions are asked when a customer is making a purchase to check any additional needs.

- Linked-selling – This is the process of recognising opportunities linked to the purchase of products. Unlike cross-selling, the customer may not have a clear need that would otherwise have been satisfied through a competitor. A good example is the Internet retailer Amazon – they stimulate additional sales by displaying other books that have also been purchased by buyers of the book that a customer is ordering.

You can also use this process when a customer attempts to order a product but you have none currently in stock. If it's a product that you normally stock, you can explain the benefits of an alternative that you do have in stock.

If it's a product that you don't normally stock, your systems should be able to record the enquiry and flag up the opportunity to consider stocking the item if it is regularly requested.

If you create good processes and systems for both winning customers and increasing the average order value you can see how much more likely you are to hit your targets.

Alternatively, it you achieve better than target for one of them it can compensate for being below target for the other.

You can take every element of your business plan and create targets in the same way. Then you can work through your processes and create or amend your systems to ensure you have the best chance of achieving those targets.

If you also continue to review your business plan and your progress towards it, you will increase your chance of succeeding.

Pitching to an investor

To find an investor who will provide more than just funding and hence overcome the Exit Catch-22 will require you to pitch your opportunity very professionally to the right type of investors.

Consider the following criteria when searching for an appropriate match between your proposal and a potential investor:

- Market sector – investors tend to stay within sectors they know.

- Channel to market – some investors only want an Internet based business others will specifically avoid this channel.

- Geographic coverage: local, national or global – some investors will only invest in a business that has the potential to scale globally.

- Level of funding required – most have a range they stay within, I know some that have virtually no lower limit, but a clear and quite modest upper limit and I know some that have a clear and significant lower limit, but virtually no upper limit.

- Exit timescale – some may be prepared to invest for a longer period, but most will look for 3 to 5 years.

The purpose of your pitch is to help an investor review the opportunity you have for success. You won't be given much time, so you have to get your message across quickly.

Most investors will be evaluating the scalability of the opportunity so your pitch should be able to convey the following aspects:

- The scale of the opportunity – you may be embarrassed to consider the scale beyond a certain level, but an investor will look at how far that could be stretched with the right level of funding. They will need to see the size of the market and the market share you believe you can achieve.

- Why you or your company has the ability to realise the opportunity – usually whatever it is that enables you to differentiate your business or products and services from the competition.

- The benefit resulting from the opportunity – usually this will be estimated alongside the exit strategy, i.e. the manner and timescale of any preferred exit.

Try to articulate the opportunity clearly and with brevity. I see many business plans without structure that take far too long to explain the opportunity and the benefit.

If you can't achieve a captivating proposal within the Executive Summary of a written document you stand no chance in a verbal pitch. An investor will make an assessment about you very rapidly.

So, you have to appeal very quickly and this is not only achieved by what you present, but most importantly by the way you present it.

Just like your business plan document, your business plan presentation requires structure. One of the benefits of a tool like PowerPoint is that it can help you devise some structure to your presentation and especially if you get nervous when presenting, it can give you a route to guide you through.

Make sure you're the centre of their attention rather than the presentation on the screen. Avoid it being too gimmicky and distracting; use it simply in a support role to your leading role.

The clearest opportunities that are quick for an investor to grasp are likely to include new Intellectual Property (IP) and may relate to one of the following:

- Product advancement – A technical or design benefit that will appeal to customers and increase your market share.

- Process advancement – A means to operate more efficiently than your competitors. Some of the gain could be passed on to customers to give a clear price advantage over the competition.

- Problem solution – A solution to a genuine problem means that customers tend to buy through necessity rather than desire. Businesses based on solutions to problems are likely to be more robust in an economic down turn.

- Expertise – A unique capability that exploits a gap in the market.

- Exclusivity – An exclusive license to market a product or service within a geographic region.

For example, the company Sightpath Limited was founded to help companies grow by modelling their business and producing all the analysis and projections discussed in this book. Therefore, this service can fit within the category of Problem Solution. But Sightpath had to make a significant investment to develop software to enable the service to be provided efficiently and hence for a reasonable price. This aspect would fit within the category of Process Advancement.

Identifying two categories like this makes it even more likely that an investor will show interest in your opportunity.

Can you identify one or more categories like those listed above for your business opportunity?

If you can, it should be delivered early within the pitch to get the audience hooked and interested enough to hear more detail.

As soon as you've told them the opportunity and how you intend to exploit it, you need to give them an estimate of scale.

They'll need to understand the size of the market and the market share that you hope to obtain within the timescale that they can expect to exit.

Then tell them how much cash you need, what you will spend it on and the level of equity on offer.

Investors will want to explore how sustainable this competitive edge is likely to remain. Explain any patents, design rights or licenses and any processes or competencies that would be difficult or costly for your competitors to acquire.

If you're unable to show the opportunity clearly and be able to demonstrate its scalability and potential, it may be that an investor is not the most appropriate way for you to finance your business.

It can take quite some time to find the right investor and you have to be able to fund your business throughout this process.

When you get the opportunity to pitch to the right kind of investor it's critical that you give yourself the best chance to impress.

Here are a few ideas to help you enhance your pitch:

- Plan – present a strong business plan including a thorough assessment of the market and competition and a detailed marketing plan. Most importantly, show them what it will mean for them. You're in competition with all the other opportunities being pitched to them.

- PR – run a high-profile PR campaign in the preceding months and collect the results in a separate binder. The credibility this can achieve can be invaluable. A client of mine managed this very successfully and has recently secured a large sum of second stage funding.

- Promotion video – make a video, for example, show satisfied customers who have become great advocates. Show how they have benefitted from your product or service. This same video may also be used in a promotional campaign to win customers.

- Practice – remember that investors are interested in you and your team and whether they can be confident that you will deliver to plan even in the face of adversity. Try to imagine all the questions they might ask and consider your responses. Rehearse your pitch to look professional and to avoid looking daunted when they ask a question you're not expecting. Get advice from wherever you can and especially from those who have been through it.

- Passion – investors love passion, it's what gets you through the inevitable set-backs they know you'll regularly encounter. They don't want to invest in someone who'll quit when the going gets tough. Give them every reason to believe in you and you're ability to pull it off. They're not trusting their cash to an opportunity or a business plan – they are trusting it to you.

Ideally, you should aim to get several investors interested at the same time to help obtain the highest investment for the lowest stake. This does not mean that you should pitch to them at the same time because a problem posed by one investor may put the other one off as well.

Just because an investor declines does not mean the opportunity is no good, it might mean your pitch had some weaknesses. Learn from each meeting – if you didn't have the answers ready for the last one, make sure you have them for the next one.

Rather like the dating game, you just have to keep searching until you find the right match.

A note of caution: Never mislead or pretend to be something you're not. The pitch is only the first stage; they will then conduct due diligence where they or their advisors will scrutinize everything. If they uncover a blatant fabrication and you lose their trust – any potential deal is likely to be terminated.

Treat each meeting with an investor as a valuable opportunity to get some free consultancy advice. Even if you don't get your hands on their cash, the insights that experienced investors can offer may significantly improve your proposition.

Summary

The chances of achieving any real success in business are disappointingly low.

This book has covered three Catch-22s that collectively conspire against an enthusiastic entrepreneur and contribute to the appalling statistics on business failure rates.

In order to grow you have to invest, but getting anyone to invest in your new business is virtually impossible unless you have a previous track record.

The odds of success are so poor that most banks and investors are not prepared to take the risk until you've already proved your proposition. This means that if you want to get your business off the ground you often have to invest your own money or cajole family or friends into backing you.

Neither you nor your friendly backers are professional investors, so the tendency is not to bother with a robust business plan that would be demanded by a professional investor. This lack of planning and professional support means that you're more likely to add to the statistics for failure.

So, because the odds are poor, the professionals will not invest, which in turn maintains the high failure rate. This is the Entry Catch-22 and relates to starting a business.

To overcome the Entry Catch-22 you have to create a business plan showing how you intend to get to a point of stability and then a professional investor or bank is more likely to back you.

Getting to the first Stability Step is best achieved by focusing on winning the required number of customers and outsourcing absolutely everything that you can.

In business there are three elements, winning it, doing it and getting paid for it. There is usually a lag between each of these, which means you need to fund the winning and the doing as well as the delay before you get paid.

If you want to grow, you'll have to spend more on winning it and then doing it, so the steeper the growth gradient – the deeper the cash requirement.

When you don't accurately predict the cash requirement for the growth gradient that you've embarked on, it will come as a surprise. After a while your cumulative cash requirement goes more negative than you expected and you feel compelled to throttle back.

You turn off your discretionary spending, which is usually the very business development initiatives that would help you grow. This leads to a sort of ladders and snakes of business and a 'saw-tooth' profile where you're expending all the effort but reaping none of the reward. If you're lucky you will flat-line, but often it puts you in a spiral of decline and you can't recover.

Your funding has to match your growth gradient, but your growth gradient depends on the funding you're able to invest – this is the Growth Catch-22.

To overcome the Growth Catch-22 you have to create a business plan with a growth gradient that maintains a balance between ambition and funding.

If you succeed enough to attract an investor for your next stage of growth you will find that your business needs to be worth much more to compensate for the equity stake you've had to relinquish. This means that you'll have to grow faster to achieve the same ambition in the same timescale, which means you'll need to invest more and therefore, give up even more equity – this is the Exit Catch-22.

To overcome the Exit Catch-22 you need to create a business plan that makes your business proposal attractive to the type of investor who can bring expertise and contacts to put you on a steeper growth gradient than you could achieve with just their investment.

To be successful, you have to break into the circularity of these three Catch-22s and overcome them. This book has given you an insight in how to do just that. It has introduced the heart of business success as a visual reminder of the importance of keeping the 3 critical 'C's: Customers, Capacity and Cash in balance as you grow.

One of the first clients I used the heart image with came back to me a few weeks later and told me how he couldn't get the image out of his mind. He thought it really helped him to visualise the structure of his business and make decisions.

The purpose of this book isn't to put you off by showing how difficult it can be to make a success of running your own business, but to help you succeed.

If it seems like an awful lot of work, let me just offer a final quote from the master of hard work and achievement, Thomas Edison: *"Opportunity is missed by most people because it's dressed in overalls and looks like work."*

But then, if you've read this far, you're probably not *most people* and I hope this book will have contributed to you joining the elite few who succeed – and always remember:

Success comes to those who plan for it AND implement it AND progress it.

If you would like further information or help about the subject of this book, please visit the following web site:

www.theheartofbusinesssuccess.com

About the author

After graduating in Physics, Robert began his career with British Aerospace as a Technical Engineer and progressed to the project management of multimillion pound, multinational contracts.

Robert then joined a subsidiary of the Rank Organisation looking after an international team of Sales and Project Managers for entertainment lighting projects.

When the company was acquired by Schroeder Ventures, Robert became Global Projects Director. During this time, he learned a great deal about how Venture Capitalists tend to operate, which has since proved invaluable when helping his clients apply for venture funding.

In 1999 Robert established Paradigm Management Consultants and clients included the UK's Ministry of Defence, but it mainly helped small companies to grow.

It was during this period that Robert became aware of the appalling failure rate of small businesses. He also discovered that most owners of small businesses believed that it was difficult to find really effective advice that was also affordable.

Robert set his mind on devising a way to deliver an effective Business Development Service at a price that was affordable to small businesses, yet was also able to generate sufficient revenues to remunerate top quality advisors.

These twin objectives seemed mutually exclusive, which mirrors the Catch-22s covered in this book. But Robert believed that if he could find a solution, he would really be able to help small businesses to become more successful and so this became his quest.

After many years and a lot of effort, as well as a substantial amount of cash, Robert and his team succeeded in developing the process and system to achieve his goal.

In 2006 Robert launched Sightpath Limited and began recruiting Business Catalysts to deliver the service. He and his team have now modelled a large number of different businesses and created many Business Development Plans. Much of the content of this book has been derived from this work.

Robert is currently still at the helm of Sightpath and speaks regularly to business groups on how to ensure they succeed. Robert is also an Expert Partner with the firm Financial Professional Support Services (FPSS).

3490636R00145

Printed in Great Britain
by Amazon.co.uk, Ltd.,
Marston Gate.